AI
Self-Driving Cars
Trendsetting

Practical Advances in
Artificial Intelligence and Machine Learning

Dr. Lance B. Eliot, MBA, PhD

DEDICATION

To my incredible daughter, Lauren, and my incredible son, Michael.

Forest fortuna adiuvat (from the Latin; good fortune favors the brave).

CONTENTS

Lance B. Eliot

ACKNOWLEDGMENTS

I have been the beneficiary of advice and counsel by many friends, colleagues, family, investors, and many others. I want to thank everyone that has aided me throughout my career. I write from the heart and the head, having experienced first-hand what it means to have others around you that support you during the good times and the tough times.

To Warren Bennis, one of my doctoral advisors and ultimately a colleague, I offer my deepest thanks and appreciation, especially for his calm and insightful wisdom and support.

To Mark Stevens and his generous efforts toward funding and supporting the USC Stevens Center for Innovation.

To Lloyd Greif and the USC Lloyd Greif Center for Entrepreneurial Studies for their ongoing encouragement of founders and entrepreneurs.

To Peter Drucker, William Wang, Aaron Levie, Peter Kim, Jon Kraft, Cindy Crawford, Jenny Ming, Steve Milligan, Chis Underwood, Frank Gehry, Buzz Aldrin, Steve Forbes, Bill Thompson, Dave Dillon, Alan Fuerstman, Larry Ellison, Jim Sinegal, John Sperling, Mark Stevenson, Anand Nallathambi, Thomas Barrack, Jr., and many other innovators and leaders that I have met and gained mightily from doing so.

Thanks to Ed Trainor, Kevin Anderson, James Hickey, Wendell Jones, Ken Harris, DuWayne Peterson, Mike Brown, Jim Thornton, Abhi Beniwal, Al Biland, John Nomura, Eliot Weinman, John Desmond, and many others for their unwavering support during my career.

And most of all thanks as always to Lauren and Michael, for their ongoing support and for having seen me writing and heard much of this material during the many months involved in writing it. To their patience and willingness to listen.

Lance B. Eliot

INTRODUCTION

This is a book that provides the newest innovations and the latest Artificial Intelligence (AI) advances about the emerging nature of AI-based autonomous self-driving driverless cars. Via recent advances in Artificial Intelligence (AI) and Machine Learning (ML), we are nearing the day when vehicles can control themselves and will not require and nor rely upon human intervention to perform their driving tasks (or, that <u>allow</u> for human intervention, but only *require* human intervention in very limited ways).

Similar to my other related books, which I describe in a moment and list the chapters in the Appendix A of this book, I am particularly focused on those advances that pertain to self-driving cars. The phrase "autonomous vehicles" is often used to refer to any kind of vehicle, whether it is ground-based or in the air or sea, and whether it is a cargo hauling trailer truck or a conventional passenger car. Though the aspects described in this book are certainly applicable to all kinds of autonomous vehicles, I am focused more so here on cars.

Indeed, I am especially known for my role in aiding the advancement of self-driving cars, serving currently as the Executive Director of the Cybernetic AI Self-Driving Cars Institute.. In addition to writing software, designing and developing systems and software for self-driving cars, I also speak and write quite a bit about the topic. This book is a collection of some of my more advanced essays. For those of you that might have seen my essays posted elsewhere, I have updated them and integrated them into this book as one handy cohesive package.

You might be interested in companion books that I have written that provide additional key innovations and fundamentals about self-driving cars. Those books are entitled **"Introduction to Driverless Self-Driving Cars," "Advances in AI and Autonomous Vehicles: Cybernetic Self-Driving Cars," "Self-Driving Cars: "The Mother of All AI Projects," "Innovation and Thought Leadership on Self-Driving Driverless Cars," "New Advances in AI Autonomous Driverless Self-Driving Cars," "Autonomous Vehicle Driverless Self-Driving Cars and Artificial Intelligence," "Transformative Artificial Intelligence**

Driverless Self-Driving Cars," "Disruptive Artificial Intelligence and Driverless Self-Driving Cars, and "State-of-the-Art AI Driverless Self-Driving Cars," and "Top Trends in AI Self-Driving Cars," and "AI Innovations and Self-Driving Cars," "Crucial Advances for AI Driverless Cars," "Sociotechnical Insights and AI Driverless Cars," "Pioneering Advances for AI Driverless Cars" and "Leading Edge Trends for AI Driverless Cars," "The Cutting Edge of AI Autonomous Cars" and "The Next Wave of AI Self-Driving Cars" and "Revolutionary Innovations of AI Self-Driving Cars," and "AI Self-Driving Cars Breakthroughs," "Trailblazing Trends for AI Self-Driving Cars," "Ingenious Strides for AI Driverless Cars," "AI Self-Driving Cars Inventiveness," "Visionary Secrets of AI Driverless Cars," "Spearheading AI Self-Driving Cars," "Spurring AI Self-Driving Cars," "Avant-Garde AI Driverless Cars," "AI Self-Driving Cars Evolvement," "AI Driverless Cars Chrysalis," "Boosting AI Autonomous Cars," "AI Self-Driving Cars Trendsetting" (they are all available via Amazon). Appendix A has a listing of the chapters covered.

For the introduction herein to this book, I am going to borrow my introduction from those companion books, since it does a good job of laying out the landscape of self-driving cars and my overall viewpoints on the topic. The remainder of the book is all new material that does not appear in the companion books.

INTRODUCTION TO SELF-DRIVING CARS

This is a book about self-driving cars. Someday in the future, we'll all have self-driving cars and this book will perhaps seem antiquated, but right now, we are at the forefront of the self-driving car wave. Daily news bombards us with flashes of new announcements by one car maker or another and leaves the impression that within the next few weeks or maybe months that the self-driving car will be here. A casual non-technical reader would assume from these news flashes that in fact we must be on the cusp of a true self-driving car. Here's a real news flash: We are still quite a distance from having a true self-driving car. It is years to go before we get there.

Why is that? Because a true self-driving car is akin to a moonshot. In the same manner that getting us to the moon was an incredible feat, likewise is achieving a true self-driving car. Anybody that suggests or even brashly states that the true self-driving car is nearly here should be viewed with great skepticism. Indeed, you'll see that I often tend to use the word "hogwash" or "crock" when I assess much of the decidedly *fake news* about self-driving cars. Those of us on the inside know that what is often reported to the outside is malarkey. Few of the insiders are willing to say so. I have no such hesitation.

Indeed, I've been writing a popular blog post about self-driving cars and hitting hard on those that try to wave their hands and pretend that we are on the imminent verge of true self-driving cars. For many years, I've been known as the AI Insider. Besides writing about AI, I also develop AI software. I do what I describe. It also gives me insights into what others that are doing AI are really doing versus what it is said they are doing.

Many faithful readers had asked me to pull together my insightful short essays and put them into another book, which you are now holding.

For those of you that have been reading my essays over the years, this collection not only puts them together into one handy package, I also updated the essays and added new material. For those of you that are new to the topic of self-driving cars and AI, I hope you find these essays approachable and informative. I also tend to have a writing style with a bit of a voice, and so you'll see that I am times have a wry sense of humor and poke at conformity.

As a former professor and founder of an AI research lab, I for many years wrote in the formal language of academic writing. I published in referred journals and served as an editor for several AI journals. This writing here is not of the nature, and I have adopted a different and more informal style for these essays. That being said, I also do mention from time-to-time more rigorous material on AI and encourage you all to dig into those deeper and more formal materials if so interested.

I am also an AI practitioner. This means that I write AI software for a living. Currently, I head-up the Cybernetics Self-Driving Car Institute, where we are developing AI software for self-driving cars. I am excited to also report that my son, also a software engineer, heads-up our Cybernetics Self-Driving Car Lab. What I have helped to start, and for which he is an integral part, ultimately he will carry long into the future after I have retired. My daughter, a marketing whiz, also is integral to our efforts as head of our Marketing group. She too will carry forward the legacy now being formulated.

For those of you that are reading this book and have a penchant for writing code, you might consider taking a look at the open source code available for self-driving cars. This is a handy place to start learning how to develop AI for self-driving cars. There are also many new educational courses spring forth. There is a growing body of those wanting to learn about and develop self-driving cars, and a growing body of colleges, labs, and other avenues by which you can learn about self-driving cars.

This book will provide a foundation of aspects that I think will get you ready for those kinds of more advanced training opportunities. If you've already taken those classes, you'll likely find these essays especially interesting as they offer a perspective that I am betting few other instructors or faculty offered to you. These are challenging essays that ask you to think beyond the conventional about self-driving cars.

THE MOTHER OF ALL AI PROJECTS

In June 2017, Apple CEO Tim Cook came out and finally admitted that Apple has been working on a self-driving car. As you'll see in my essays, Apple was enmeshed in secrecy about their self-driving car efforts. We have only been able to read the tea leaves and guess at what Apple has been up to. The notion of an iCar has been floating for quite a while, and self-driving engineers and researchers have been signing tight-lipped Non-Disclosure Agreements (NDA's) to work on projects at Apple that were as shrouded in mystery as any military invasion plans might be.

Tim Cook said something that many others in the Artificial Intelligence (AI) field have been saying, namely, the creation of a self-driving car has got to be the mother of all AI projects. In other words, it is in fact a tremendous moonshot for AI. If a self-driving car can be crafted and the AI works as we hope, it means that we have made incredible strides with AI and that therefore it opens many other worlds of potential breakthrough accomplishments that AI can solve.

Is this hyperbole? Am I just trying to make AI seem like a miracle worker and so provide self-aggrandizing statements for those of us writing the AI software for self-driving cars? No, it is not hyperbole. Developing a true self-driving car is really, really, really hard to do. Let me take a moment to explain why. As a side note, I realize that the Apple CEO is known for at times uttering hyperbole, and he had previously said for example that the year 2012 was "the mother of all years," and he had said that the release of iOS 10 was "the mother of all releases" – all of which does suggest he likes to use the handy "mother of" expression. But, I assure you, in terms of true self-driving cars, he has hit the nail on the head. For sure.

When you think about a moonshot and how we got to the moon, there are some identifiable characteristics and those same aspects can be applied to creating a true self-driving car. You'll notice that I keep putting the word "true" in front of the self-driving car expression. I do so because as per my essay about the various levels of self-driving cars, there are some self-driving cars that are only somewhat of a self-driving car. The somewhat versions are ones that require a human driver to be ready to intervene. In my view, that's not a true self-driving car. A true self-driving car is one that requires no human driver intervention at all. It is a car that can entirely undertake via automation the driving task without any human driver needed. This is the essence of what is known as a Level 5 self-driving car. We are currently at the Level 2 and Level 3 mark, and not yet at Level 5.

Getting to the moon involved aspects such as having big stretch goals, incremental progress, experimentation, innovation, and so on. Let's review how this applied to the moonshot of the bygone era, and how it applies to the self-driving car moonshot of today.

Big Stretch Goal

Trying to take a human and deliver the human to the moon, and bring them back, safely, was an extremely large stretch goal at the time. No one knew whether it could be done. The technology wasn't available yet. The cost was huge. The determination would need to be fierce. Etc. To reach a Level 5 self-driving car is going to be the same. It is a big stretch goal. We can readily get to the Level 3, and we are able to see the Level 4 just up ahead, but a Level 5 is still an unknown as to if it is doable. It should eventually be doable and in the same way that we thought we'd eventually get to the moon, but when it will occur is a different story.

Incremental Progress

Getting to the moon did not happen overnight in one fell swoop. It took years and years of incremental progress to get there. Likewise for self-driving cars. Google has famously been striving to get to the Level 5, and pretty much been willing to forgo dealing with the intervening levels, but most of the other self-driving car makers are doing the incremental route. Let's get a good Level 2 and a somewhat Level 3 going. Then, let's improve the Level 3 and get a somewhat Level 4 going. Then, let's improve the Level 4 and finally arrive at a Level 5. This seems to be the prevalent way that we are going to achieve the true self-driving car.

Experimentation

You likely know that there were various experiments involved in perfecting the approach and technology to get to the moon. As per making incremental progress, we first tried to see if we could get a rocket to go into space and safety return, then put a monkey in there, then with a human, then we went all the way to the moon but didn't land, and finally we arrived at the mission that actually landed on the moon. Self-driving cars are the same way. We are doing simulations of self-driving cars. We do testing of self-driving cars on private land under controlled situations. We do testing of self-driving cars on public roadways, often having to meet regulatory requirements including for example having an engineer or equivalent in the car to take over the controls if needed. And so on. Experiments big and small are needed to figure out what works and what doesn't.

Innovation

There are already some advances in AI that are allowing us to progress toward self-driving cars. We are going to need even more advances. Innovation in all aspects of technology are going to be required to achieve a true self-driving car. By no means do we already have everything in-hand that we need to get there. Expect new inventions and new approaches, new algorithms, etc.

Setbacks

Most of the pundits are avoiding talking about potential setbacks in the progress toward self-driving cars. Getting to the moon involved many setbacks, some of which you never have heard of and were buried at the time so as to not dampen enthusiasm and funding for getting to the moon. A recurring theme in many of my included essays is that there are going to be setbacks as we try to arrive at a true self-driving car. Take a deep breath and be ready. I just hope the setbacks don't completely stop progress. I am sure that it will cause progress to alter in a manner that we've not yet seen in the self-driving car field. I liken the self-driving car of today to the excitement everyone had for Uber when it first got going. Today, we have a different view of Uber and with each passing day there are more regulations to the ride sharing business and more concerns raised. The darling child only stays a darling until finally that child acts up. It will happen the same with self-driving cars.

SELF-DRIVING CARS CHALLENGES

But what exactly makes things so hard to have a true self-driving car, you might be asking. You have seen cruise control for years and years. You've lately seen cars that can do parallel parking. You've seen YouTube videos of Tesla drivers that put their hands out the window as their car zooms along the highway, and seen to therefore be in a self-driving car. Aren't we just needing to put a few more sensors onto a car and then we'll have in-hand a true self-driving car? Nope.

Consider for a moment the nature of the driving task. We don't just let anyone at any age drive a car. Worldwide, most countries won't license a driver until the age of 18, though many do allow a learner's permit at the age of 15 or 16. Some suggest that a younger age would be physically too small to reach the controls of the car. Though this might be the case, we could easily adjust the controls to allow for younger aged and thus smaller stature. It's not their physical size that matters. It's their cognitive development that matters.

To drive a car, you need to be able to reason about the car, what the car can and cannot do. You need to know how to operate the car. You need to know about how other cars on the road drive. You need to know what is allowed in driving such as speed limits and driving within marked lanes. You need to be able to react to situations and be able to avoid getting into accidents. You need to ascertain when to hit your brakes, when to steer clear of a pedestrian, and how to keep from ramming that motorcyclist that just cut you off.

Many of us had taken courses on driving. We studied about driving and took driver training. We had to take a test and pass it to be able to drive. The point being that though most adults take the driving task for granted, and we often "mindlessly" drive our cars, there is a significant amount of cognitive effort that goes into driving a car. After a while, it becomes second nature. You don't especially think about how you drive, you just do it. But, if you watch a novice driver, say a teenager learning to drive, you suddenly realize that there is a lot more complexity to it than we seem to realize.

Furthermore, driving is a very serious task. I recall when my daughter and son first learned to drive. They are both very conscientious people. They wanted to make sure that whatever they did, they did well, and that they did not harm anyone. Every day, when you get into a car, it is probably around 4,000 pounds of hefty metal and plastics (about two tons), and it is a lethal weapon. Think about it. You drive down the street in an object that weighs two tons and with the engine it can accelerate and ram into anything you want to hit. The damage a car can inflict is very scary. Both my children were surprised that they were being given the right to maneuver this monster of a beast that could cause tremendous harm entirely by merely letting go of the steering wheel for a moment or taking your eyes off the road.

In fact, in the United States alone there are about 30,000 deaths per year by auto accidents, which is around 100 per day. Given that there are about 263 million cars in the United States, I am actually more amazed that the number of fatalities is not a lot higher. During my morning commute, I look at all the thousands of cars on the freeway around me, and I think that if all of them decided to go zombie and drive in a crazy maniac way, there would be many people dead. Somehow, incredibly, each day, most people drive relatively safely. To me, that's a miracle right there. Getting millions and millions of people to be safe and sane when behind the wheel of a two ton mobile object, it's a feat that we as a society should admire with pride.

So, hopefully you are in agreement that the driving task requires a great deal of cognition. You don't' need to be especially smart to drive a car, and we've done quite a bit to make car driving viable for even the average dolt. There isn't an IQ test that you need to take to drive a car. If you can read and write, and pass a test, you pretty much can legally drive a car. There are of course some that drive a car and are not legally permitted to do so, plus there are private areas such as farms where drivers are young, but for public roadways in the United States, you can be generally of average intelligence (or less) and be able to legally drive.

This though makes it seem like the cognitive effort must not be much. If the cognitive effort was truly hard, wouldn't we only have Einstein's that could drive a car? We have made sure to keep the driving task as simple as we can, by making the controls easy and relatively standardized, and by having roads that are relatively standardized, and so on. It is as though Disneyland has put their Autopia into the real-world, by us all as a society agreeing that roads will be a certain way, and we'll all abide by the various rules of driving.

A modest cognitive task by a human is still something that stymies AI. You certainly know that AI has been able to beat chess players and be good at other kinds of games. This type of narrow cognition is not what car driving is about. Car driving is much wider. It requires knowledge about the world, which a chess playing AI system does not need to know. The cognitive aspects of driving are on the one hand seemingly simple, but at the same time require layer upon layer of knowledge about cars, people, roads, rules, and a myriad of other "common sense" aspects. We don't have any AI systems today that have that same kind of breadth and depth of awareness and knowledge.

As revealed in my essays, the self-driving car of today is using trickery to do particular tasks. It is all very narrow in operation. Plus, it currently assumes that a human driver is ready to intervene. It is like a child that we have taught to stack blocks, but we are needed to be right there in case the child stacks them too high and they begin to fall over. AI of today is brittle, it is narrow, and it does not approach the cognitive abilities of humans. This is why the true self-driving car is somewhere out in the future.

Another aspect to the driving task is that it is not solely a mind exercise. You do need to use your senses to drive. You use your eyes a vision sensors to see the road ahead. You vision capability is like a streaming video, which your brain needs to continually analyze as you drive. Where is the road? Is there a pedestrian in the way? Is there another car ahead of you? Your senses are relying a flood of info to your brain. Self-driving cars are trying to do the same, by using cameras, radar, ultrasound, and lasers. This is an attempt at mimicking how humans have senses and sensory apparatus.

Thus, the driving task is mental and physical. You use your senses, you use your arms and legs to manipulate the controls of the car, and you use your brain to assess the sensory info and direct your limbs to act upon the controls of the car. This all happens instantly. If you've ever perhaps gotten something in your eye and only had one eye available to drive with, you suddenly realize how dependent upon vision you are. If you have a broken foot with a cast, you suddenly realize how hard it is to control the brake pedal and the accelerator. If you've taken medication and your brain is maybe sluggish, you suddenly realize how much mental strain is required to drive a car.

An AI system that plays chess only needs to be focused on playing chess. The physical aspects aren't important because usually a human moves the chess pieces or the chessboard is shown on an electronic display. Using AI for a more life-and-death task such as analyzing MRI images of patients, this again does not require physical capabilities and instead is done by examining images of bits.

Driving a car is a true life-and-death task. It is a use of AI that can easily and at any moment produce death. For those colleagues of mine that are developing this AI, as am I, we need to keep in mind the somber aspects of this. We are producing software that will have in its virtual hands the lives of the occupants of the car, and the lives of those in other nearby cars, and the lives of nearby pedestrians, etc. Chess is not usually a life-or-death matter.

Driving is all around us. Cars are everywhere. Most of today's AI applications involve only a small number of people. Or, they are behind the scenes and we as humans have other recourse if the AI messes up. AI that is driving a car at 80 miles per hour on a highway had better not mess up. The consequences are grave. Multiply this by the number of cars, if we could put magically self-driving into every car in the USA, we'd have AI running in the 263 million cars. That's a lot of AI spread around. This is AI on a massive scale that we are not doing today and that offers both promise and potential peril.

There are some that want AI for self-driving cars because they envision a world without any car accidents. They envision a world in which there is no car congestion and all cars cooperate with each other. These are wonderful utopian visions.

They are also very misleading. The adoption of self-driving cars is going to be incremental and not overnight. We cannot economically just junk all existing cars. Nor are we going to be able to affordably retrofit existing cars. It is more likely that self-driving cars will be built into new cars and that over many years of gradual replacement of existing cars that we'll see the mix of self-driving cars become substantial in the real-world.

In these essays, I have tried to offer technological insights without being overly technical in my description, and also blended the business, societal, and economic aspects too. Technologists need to consider the non-technological impacts of what they do. Non-technologists should be aware of what is being developed.

We all need to work together to collectively be prepared for the enormous disruption and transformative aspects of true self-driving cars. We all need to be involved in this mother of all AI projects.

WHAT THIS BOOK PROVIDES

What does this book provide to you? It introduces many of the key elements about self-driving cars and does so with an AI based perspective. I weave together technical and non-technical aspects, readily going from being concerned about the cognitive capabilities of the driving task and how the technology is embodying this into self-driving cars, and in the next breath I discuss the societal and economic aspects.

They are all intertwined because that's the way reality is. You cannot separate out the technology per se, and instead must consider it within the milieu of what is being invented and innovated, and do so with a mindset towards the contemporary mores and culture that shape what we are doing and what we hope to do.

WHY THIS BOOK

I wrote this book to try and bring to the public view many aspects about self-driving cars that nobody seems to be discussing.

For business leaders that are either involved in making self-driving cars or that are going to leverage self-driving cars, I hope that this book will enlighten you as to the risks involved and ways in which you should be strategizing about how to deal with those risks.

For entrepreneurs, startups and other businesses that want to enter into the self-driving car market that is emerging, I hope this book sparks your interest in doing so, and provides some sense of what might be prudent to pursue.

For researchers that study self-driving cars, I hope this book spurs your interest in the risks and safety issues of self-driving cars, and also nudges you toward conducting research on those aspects.

For students in computer science or related disciplines, I hope this book will provide you with interesting and new ideas and material, for which you might conduct research or provide some career direction insights for you.

For AI companies and high-tech companies pursuing self-driving cars, this book will hopefully broaden your view beyond just the mere coding and development needed to make self-driving cars.

For all readers, I hope that you will find the material in this book to be stimulating. Some of it will be repetitive of things you already know. But I am pretty sure that you'll also find various eureka moments whereby you'll discover a new technique or approach that you had not earlier thought of. I am also betting that there will be material that forces you to rethink some of your current practices.

I am not saying you will suddenly have an epiphany and change what you are doing. I do think though that you will reconsider or perhaps revisit what you are doing.

For anyone choosing to use this book for teaching purposes, please take a look at my suggestions for doing so, as described in the Appendix. I have found the material handy in courses that I have taught, and likewise other faculty have told me that they have found the material handy, in some cases as extended readings and in other instances as a core part of their course (depending on the nature of the class).

In my writing for this book, I have tried carefully to blend both the practitioner and the academic styles of writing. It is not as dense as is typical academic journal writing, but at the same time offers depth by going into the nuances and trade-offs of various practices.

The word "deep" is in vogue today, meaning getting deeply into a subject or topic, and so is the word "unpack" which means to tease out the underlying aspects of a subject or topic. I have sought to offer material that addresses an issue or topic by going relatively deeply into it and make sure that it is well unpacked.

In any book about AI, it is difficult to use our everyday words without having some of them be misinterpreted. Specifically, it is easy to anthropomorphize AI. When I say that an AI system "knows" something, I do not want you to construe that the AI system has sentience and "knows" in the same way that humans do. They aren't that way, as yet. I have tried to use quotes around such words from time-to-time to emphasize that the words I am using should not be misinterpreted to ascribe true human intelligence to the AI systems that we know of today. If I used quotes around all such words, the book would be very difficult to read, and so I am doing so judiciously. Please keep that in mind as you read the material, thanks.

Some of the material is time-based in terms of covering underway activities, and though some of it might decay, nonetheless I believe you'll find the material useful and informative.

COMPANION BOOKS

1. **"Introduction to Driverless Self-Driving Cars"** by Dr. Lance Eliot

2. **"Innovation and Thought Leadership on Self-Driving Driverless Cars"** by Dr. Lance Eliot

3. **"Advances in AI and Autonomous Vehicles: Cybernetic Self-Driving Cars"** by Dr. Lance Eliot

4. **"Self-Driving Cars: The Mother of All AI Projects"** by Dr. Lance Eliot

5. **"New Advances in AI Autonomous Driverless Self-Driving Cars"** by Dr. Lance Eliot

6. **"Autonomous Vehicle Driverless Self-Driving Cars and Artificial Intelligence"** by Dr. Lance Eliot and Michael B. Eliot

7. **"Transformative Artificial Intelligence Driverless Self-Driving Cars"** by Dr. Lance Eliot

8. **"Disruptive Artificial Intelligence and Driverless Self-Driving Cars"** by Dr. Lance Eliot

9. "State-of-the-Art AI Driverless Self-Driving Cars" by Dr. Lance Eliot

10. "Top Trends in AI Self-Driving Cars" by Dr. Lance Eliot

11. **"AI Innovations and Self-Driving Cars"** by Dr. Lance Eliot

12. **"Crucial Advances for AI Driverless Cars"** by Dr. Lance Eliot

13. **"Sociotechnical Insights and AI Driverless Cars"** by Dr. Lance Eliot.

14. **"Pioneering Advances for AI Driverless Cars"** by Dr. Lance Eliot

15. **"Leading Edge Trends for AI Driverless Cars"** by Dr. Lance Eliot

16. **"The Cutting Edge of AI Autonomous Cars"** by Dr. Lance Eliot

17. **"The Next Wave of AI Self-Driving Cars"** by Dr. Lance Eliot

18. **"Revolutionary Innovations of AI Driverless Cars"** by Dr. Lance Eliot

19. **"AI Self-Driving Cars Breakthroughs"** by Dr. Lance Eliot

20. **"Trailblazing Trends for AI Self-Driving Cars"** by Dr. Lance Eliot

21. **"Ingenious Strides for AI Driverless Cars"** by Dr. Lance Eliot

22. **"AI Self-Driving Cars Inventiveness"** by Dr. Lance Eliot

23. **"Visionary Secrets of AI Driverless Cars"** by Dr. Lance Eliot

24. **"Spearheading AI Self-Driving Cars"** by Dr. Lance Eliot

25. **"Spurring AI Self-Driving Cars"** by Dr. Lance Eliot

26. **"Avant-Garde AI Driverless Cars"** by Dr. Lance Eliot

27. **"AI Self-Driving Cars Evolvement"** by Dr. Lance Eliot

28. **"AI Driverless Cars Chrysalis"** by Dr. Lance Eliot

29. **"Boosting AI Autonomous Cars"** by Dr. Lance Eliot

30. **"AI Self-Driving Cars Trendsetting"** by Dr. Lance Eliot

These books are available on Amazon and at other major global booksellers.

CHAPTER 1

ELIOT FRAMEWORK FOR AI SELF-DRIVING CARS

CHAPTER 1

ELIOT FRAMEWORK FOR AI SELF-DRIVING CARS

This chapter is a core foundational aspect for understanding AI self-driving cars and I have used this same chapter in several of my other books to introduce the reader to essential elements of this field. Once you've read this chapter, you'll be prepared to read the rest of the material since the foundational essence of the components of autonomous AI driverless self-driving cars will have been established for you.

––––––––––

When I give presentations about self-driving cars and teach classes on the topic, I have found it helpful to provide a framework around which the various key elements of self-driving cars can be understood and organized (see diagram at the end of this chapter). The framework needs to be simple enough to convey the overarching elements, but at the same time not so simple that it belies the true complexity of self-driving cars. As such, I am going to describe the framework here and try to offer in a thousand words (or more!) what the framework diagram itself intends to portray.

The core elements on the diagram are numbered for ease of reference. The numbering does not suggest any kind of prioritization of the elements. Each element is crucial. Each element has a purpose, and otherwise would not be included in the framework. For some self-driving cars, a particular element might be more important or somehow distinguished in comparison to other self-driving cars.

You could even use the framework to rate a particular self-driving car, doing so by gauging how well it performs in each of the elements of the framework. I will describe each of the elements, one at a time. After doing so, I'll discuss aspects that illustrate how the elements interact and perform during the overall effort of a self-driving car.

At the Cybernetic Self-Driving Car Institute, we use the framework to keep track of what we are working on, and how we are developing software that fills in what is needed to achieve Level 5 self-driving cars.

D-01: Sensor Capture

Let's start with the one element that often gets the most attention in the press about self-driving cars, namely, the sensory devices for a self-driving car.

On the framework, the box labeled as D-01 indicates "Sensor Capture" and refers to the processes of the self-driving car that involve collecting data from the myriad of sensors that are used for a self-driving car. The types of devices typically involved are listed, such as the use of mono cameras, stereo cameras, LIDAR devices, radar systems, ultrasonic devices, GPS, IMU, and so on.

These devices are tasked with obtaining data about the status of the self-driving car and the world around it. Some of the devices are continually providing updates, while others of the devices await an indication by the self-driving car that the device is supposed to collect data. The data might be first transformed in some fashion by the device itself, or it might instead be fed directly into the sensor capture as raw data. At that point, it might be up to the sensor capture processes to do transformations on the data. This all varies depending upon the nature of the devices being used and how the devices were designed and developed.

D-02: Sensor Fusion

Imagine that your eyeballs receive visual images, your nose receives odors, your ears receive sounds, and in essence each of your distinct sensory devices is getting some form of input. The input befits the nature of the device. Likewise, for a self-driving car, the cameras provide visual images, the radar returns radar reflections, and so on.

Each device provides the data as befits what the device does.

At some point, using the analogy to humans, you need to merge together what your eyes see, what your nose smells, what your ears hear, and piece it all together into a larger sense of what the world is all about and what is happening around you. Sensor fusion is the action of taking the singular aspects from each of the devices and putting them together into a larger puzzle.

Sensor fusion is a tough task. There are some devices that might not be working at the time of the sensor capture. Or, there might some devices that are unable to report well what they have detected. Again, using a human analogy, suppose you are in a dark room and so your eyes cannot see much. At that point, you might need to rely more so on your ears and what you hear. The same is true for a self-driving car. If the cameras are obscured due to snow and sleet, it might be that the radar can provide a greater indication of what the external conditions consist of.

In the case of a self-driving car, there can be a plethora of such sensory devices. Each is reporting what it can. Each might have its difficulties. Each might have its limitations, such as how far ahead it can detect an object. All of these limitations need to be considered during the sensor fusion task.

D-03: Virtual World Model

For humans, we presumably keep in our minds a model of the world around us when we are driving a car. In your mind, you know that the car is going at say 60 miles per hour and that you are on a freeway. You have a model in your mind that your car is surrounded by other cars, and that there are lanes to the freeway. Your model is not only based on what you can see, hear, etc., but also what you know about the nature of the world. You know that at any moment that car ahead of you can smash on its brakes, or the car behind you can ram into your car, or that the truck in the next lane might swerve into your lane.

The AI of the self-driving car needs to have a virtual world model, which it then keeps updated with whatever it is receiving from the sensor fusion, which received its input from the sensor capture and the sensory devices.

D-04: System Action Plan

By having a virtual world model, the AI of the self-driving car is able to keep track of where the car is and what is happening around the car. In addition, the AI needs to determine what to do next. Should the self-driving car hit its brakes? Should the self-driving car stay in its lane or swerve into the lane to the left? Should the self-driving car accelerate or slow down?

A system action plan needs to be prepared by the AI of the self-driving car. The action plan specifies what actions should be taken. The actions need to pertain to the status of the virtual world model. Plus, the actions need to be realizable.

This realizability means that the AI cannot just assert that the self-driving car should suddenly sprout wings and fly. Instead, the AI must be bound by whatever the self-driving car can actually do, such as coming to a halt in a distance of X feet at a speed of Y miles per hour, rather than perhaps asserting that the self-driving car come to a halt in 0 feet as though it could instantaneously come to a stop while it is in motion.

D-05: Controls Activation

The system action plan is implemented by activating the controls of the car to act according to what the plan stipulates. This might mean that the accelerator control is commanded to increase the speed of the car. Or, the steering control is commanded to turn the steering wheel 30 degrees to the left or right.

One question arises as to whether or not the controls respond as they are commanded to do. In other words, suppose the AI has commanded the accelerator to increase, but for some reason it does not do so. Or, maybe it tries to do so, but the speed of the car does not increase. The controls activation feeds back into the virtual world model, and simultaneously the virtual world model is getting updated from the sensors, the sensor capture, and the sensor fusion. This allows the AI to ascertain what has taken place as a result of the controls being commanded to take some kind of action.

By the way, please keep in mind that though the diagram seems to have a linear progression to it, the reality is that these are all aspects of the self-driving car that are happening in parallel and simultaneously. The sensors are capturing data, meanwhile the sensor fusion is taking place, meanwhile the virtual model is being updated, meanwhile the system action plan is being formulated and reformulated, meanwhile the controls are being activated.

This is the same as a human being that is driving a car. They are eyeballing the road, meanwhile they are fusing in their mind the sights, sounds, etc., meanwhile their mind is updating their model of the world around them, meanwhile they are formulating an action plan of what to do, and meanwhile they are pushing their foot onto the pedals and steering the car. In the normal course of driving a car, you are doing all of these at once. I mention this so that when you look at the diagram, you will think of the boxes as processes that are all happening at the same time, and not as though only one happens and then the next.

They are shown diagrammatically in a simplistic manner to help comprehend what is taking place. You though should also realize that they are working in parallel and simultaneous with each other. This is a tough aspect in that the inter-element communications involve latency and other aspects that must be taken into account. There can be delays in one element updating and then sharing its latest status with other elements.

D-06: Automobile & CAN

Contemporary cars use various automotive electronics and a Controller Area Network (CAN) to serve as the components that underlie the driving aspects of a car. There are Electronic Control Units (ECU's) which control subsystems of the car, such as the engine, the brakes, the doors, the windows, and so on.

The elements D-01, D-02, D-03, D-04, D-05 are layered on top of the D-06, and must be aware of the nature of what the D-06 is able to do and not do.

D-07: In-Car Commands

Humans are going to be occupants in self-driving cars. In a Level 5 self-driving car, there must be some form of communication that takes place between the humans and the self-driving car. For example, I go into a self-driving car and tell it that I want to be driven over to Disneyland, and along the way I want to stop at In-and-Out Burger. The self-driving car now parses what I've said and tries to then establish a means to carry out my wishes.

In-car commands can happen at any time during a driving journey. Though my example was about an in-car command when I first got into my self-driving car, it could be that while the self-driving car is carrying out the journey that I change my mind. Perhaps after getting stuck in traffic, I tell the self-driving car to forget about getting the burgers and just head straight over to the theme park. The self-driving car needs to be alert to in-car commands throughout the journey.

D-08: V2X Communications

We will ultimately have self-driving cars communicating with each other, doing so via V2V (Vehicle-to-Vehicle) communications. We will also have self-driving cars that communicate with the roadways and other aspects of the transportation infrastructure, doing so via V2I (Vehicle-to-Infrastructure).

The variety of ways in which a self-driving car will be communicating with other cars and infrastructure is being called V2X, whereby the letter X means whatever else we identify as something that a car should or would want to communicate with. The V2X communications will be taking place simultaneous with everything else on the diagram, and those other elements will need to incorporate whatever it gleans from those V2X communications.

D-09: Deep Learning

The use of Deep Learning permeates all other aspects of the self-driving car. The AI of the self-driving car will be using deep learning to do a better job at the systems action plan, and at the controls activation, and at the sensor fusion, and so on.

Currently, the use of artificial neural networks is the most prevalent form of deep learning. Based on large swaths of data, the neural networks attempt to "learn" from the data and therefore direct the efforts of the self-driving car accordingly.

D-10: Tactical AI

Tactical AI is the element of dealing with the moment-to-moment driving of the self-driving car. Is the self-driving car staying in its lane of the freeway? Is the car responding appropriately to the controls commands? Are the sensory devices working?

For human drivers, the tactical equivalent can be seen when you watch a novice driver such as a teenager that is first driving. They are focused on the mechanics of the driving task, keeping their eye on the road while also trying to properly control the car.

D-11: Strategic AI

The Strategic AI aspects of a self-driving car are dealing with the larger picture of what the self-driving car is trying to do. If I had asked that the self-driving car take me to Disneyland, there is an overall journey map that needs to be kept and maintained.

There is an interaction between the Strategic AI and the Tactical AI. The Strategic AI is wanting to keep on the mission of the driving, while the Tactical AI is focused on the particulars underway in the driving effort. If the Tactical AI seems to wander away from the overarching mission, the Strategic AI wants to see why and get things back on track. If the Tactical AI realizes that there is something amiss on the self-driving car, it needs to alert the Strategic AI accordingly and have an adjustment to the overarching mission that is underway.

D-12: Self-Aware AI

Very few of the self-driving cars being developed are including a Self-Aware AI element, which we at the Cybernetic Self-Driving Car Institute believe is crucial to Level 5 self-driving cars.

The Self-Aware AI element is intended to watch over itself, in the sense that the AI is making sure that the AI is working as intended. Suppose you had a human driving a car, and they were starting to drive erratically. Hopefully, their own self-awareness would make them realize they themselves are driving poorly, such as perhaps starting to fall asleep after having been driving for hours on end. If you had a passenger in the car, they might be able to alert the driver if the driver is starting to do something amiss. This is exactly what the Self-Aware

AI element tries to do, it becomes the overseer of the AI, and tries to detect when the AI has become faulty or confused, and then find ways to overcome the issue.

D-13: Economic

The economic aspects of a self-driving car are not per se a technology aspect of a self-driving car, but the economics do indeed impact the nature of a self-driving car. For example, the cost of outfitting a self-driving car with every kind of possible sensory device is prohibitive, and so choices need to be made about which devices are used. And, for those sensory devices chosen, whether they would have a full set of features or a more limited set of features.

We are going to have self-driving cars that are at the low-end of a consumer cost point, and others at the high-end of a consumer cost point. You cannot expect that the self-driving car at the low-end is going to be as robust as the one at the high-end. I realize that many of the self-driving car pundits are acting as though all self-driving cars will be the same, but they won't be. Just like anything else, we are going to have self-driving cars that have a range of capabilities. Some will be better than others. Some will be safer than others. This is the way of the real-world, and so we need to be thinking about the economics aspects when considering the nature of self-driving cars.

D-14: Societal

This component encompasses the societal aspects of AI which also impacts the technology of self-driving cars. For example, the famous Trolley Problem involves what choices should a self-driving car make when faced with life-and-death matters. If the self-driving car is about to either hit a child standing in the roadway, or instead ram into a tree at the side of the road and possibly kill the humans in the self-driving car, which choice should be made?

We need to keep in mind the societal aspects will underlie the AI of the self-driving car. Whether we are aware of it explicitly or not, the AI will have embedded into it various societal assumptions.

D-15: Innovation

I included the notion of innovation into the framework because we can anticipate that whatever a self-driving car consists of, it will continue to be innovated over time. The self-driving cars coming out in the next several years will undoubtedly be different and less innovative than the versions that come out in ten years hence, and so on.

Framework Overall

For those of you that want to learn about self-driving cars, you can potentially pick a particular element and become specialized in that aspect. Some engineers are focusing on the sensory devices. Some engineers focus on the controls activation. And so on. There are specialties in each of the elements.

Researchers are likewise specializing in various aspects. For example, there are researchers that are using Deep Learning to see how best it can be used for sensor fusion. There are other researchers that are using Deep Learning to derive good System Action Plans. Some are studying how to develop AI for the Strategic aspects of the driving task, while others are focused on the Tactical aspects.

A well-prepared all-around software developer that is involved in self-driving cars should be familiar with all of the elements, at least to the degree that they know what each element does. This is important since whatever piece of the pie that the software developer works on, they need to be knowledgeable about what the other elements are doing.

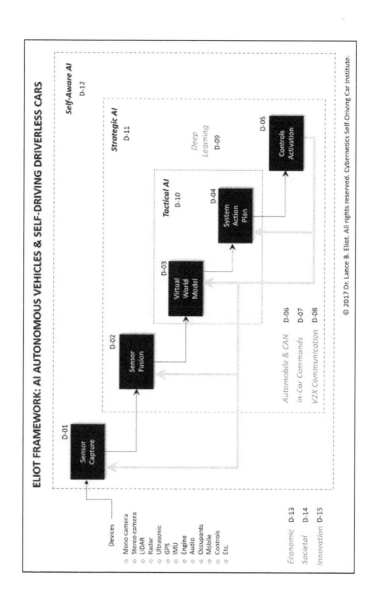

ELIOT FRAMEWORK: AI AUTONOMOUS VEHICLES & SELF-DRIVING DRIVERLESS CARS

CHAPTER 2
OTA MYTHS
AND
AI SELF-DRIVING CARS

CHAPTER 2

OTA MYTHS
AND AI SELF-DRIVING CARS

Getting an update to your smartphone or laptop computer via an Over-The-Air (OTA) capability is akin to a box of chocolates, you never know exactly what you're gonna get. The vaunted ability to electronically beam changes to your electronic devices does offer some quite nifty advantages, but we need to recognize and acknowledge the downsides of such immediacy of making alterations to any complex system.

The loudly touted advantages of using OTA for a multi-ton autonomous driverless car needs to be offset by the fact that the traffic-going vehicle involves true life-or-death consequences. Bricking or messing up your smartphone is annoying but not life-threatening while putting something new and perhaps adverse into your self-driving car could be untoward or outright deadly.

We are entering into the age of high fluidity or plasticity, allowing complex systems to be nimbly updated, reducing the friction of having to make updates, yet with this rapidity there is also increased risks of making tweaks that go too far, inadvertently, leading to noxious consequences.

OTA And Dealership-Customer Impacts

An alluring element of the so-called "software upgradable car" is the ease of having the automaker provide you with the latest added features or revised capabilities, doing so remotely, presumably at a time and place of your choosing. No more having to schlep your car over to the dealership, which likely required taking time out of your day that you don't have and waiting around endlessly as some automotive technician plugged a USB stick into a port on your car and manually installed updates to the vehicle software.

Dealers aren't necessarily fully enamored of the remote OTA capability.

For many dealers, the need for you to come into to do maintenance on your car was a ripe opportunity to get to know you, creating perhaps a stronger bond with a customer who might, later on, want a newer car or have other needs. In that sense, OTA is taking opportunistic money away from the dealer. Admittedly, the visit to the dealer for software updates also created an upsell opening too, gauging whether you might like something else done for your car while you are there anyway.

Some though worry that the advent of OTA is going to worsen the procrastination of many car owners.

According to stats by the National Highway Traffic Safety Administration, or NHTSA, an astounding 60% of automotive recalls go unaccomplished, meaning that there are a lot of cars on our roadways that have a known defect and yet are still driving among you and me.

Fixing the recalled item is not just about the safety of that particular car and its driver, but frequently also about the safety of all other cars and pedestrians that might be nearby to that defective car.

It seems logical to assume that car owners will be even less likely to get their automobile's physical-parts recalls undertaken when there is no longer a need to go to the dealership due to the OTA aspects. You often opt to get a recall item fixed or replaced when you otherwise were at the dealership, now, those odds are lessened.

Dealers too have reported that when OTAs are being performed remotely, while someone's car sits in their garage at home, the dealership at times get phone calls from their customers as to what the OTA consists of. Unfortunately, there often is a knowledge gap between what the automaker is pushing out via their OTA cloud to the vehicles, and what the local dealership knows about it. This can be confounding to customers and make dealerships look peculiarly out-of-the-loop and unaware.

OTA Is Both A Blessing And A Curse

Perhaps more disconcerting is the nature of the updates that the OTA is doing to your car.

The ease of the automaker to push out new changes to your car's systems can add intense and at times unrelenting pressure to the automotive engineers devising the updates, based on now-heightened customer expectations that any wishfully desired capability can be readily transmitted into their cars, right away and at the push of a button. Car owners start a tweet storm about some aspect of their car that they don't like or wish to have changed, and all of a sudden, the clock is ticking on getting that latest update sent out via OTA.

One notable example of a quick fix might be the Consumer Reports (CR) aspect last year in May, when CR indicated that the braking distance performance of the Tesla Model 3 was worse than a Ford F-150, and Elon Musk tweeted out that this could be resolved quickly, and a few days later an OTA was remotely pushed out by Tesla that lopped 19 feet off the stopping distance (CR then revised their scoring and recommended the car).

This kind of rapidity can seem on the surface like a blessing. There is also the curse side of that coin too.

OTA Box of Chocolates

Let's consider some overarching aspects of driverless cars and the OTA box of chocolates:

• Will the rather immediate OTA updates get their due in terms of proper testing, or will there be a short-shrift when the pressure is on to get something out-the-door right away?

Ironically, the old way, the more logistically sluggish process, actually allowed for a more measured review of what is to be changed and what impacts it might have.

• Will customers understand what the OTA changes did to the car and be able to adjust their own driving practices accordingly?

For self-driving cars less than a true Level 5 autonomous car, there must be a human driver that co-shares the driving with the automation. When the automation suddenly changes overnight, the human driver might be surprised or taken aback when the car suddenly reacts or undertakes a different driving tactic than it did the day before. That person might make a mistake and the delicate dance between the car's ADAS (Advanced Driver-Assistance Systems) capabilities and human driver falls apart, injuriously.

• Will there be changes done via an OTA to fix some otherwise latent issue, one that consumers are in-the-dark about?

Suppose that an automaker realizes there is a defect in their car, and it can be overcome by a software change. Meanwhile, those that use that car had been exposed to the defect and might have even gotten into car accidents because of it.

By slipping the fix into the OTA stream, consumers will not know they had been earlier at risk and that the problem could have been the fault that led to a car wreck or incident. OTA can hide something that otherwise the automaker might have been forced to reveal.

• Will a software update via OTA be inaptly used to cope with an actual hardware or car parts issue?

If there is a component on your autonomous car that was poorly made or has some significant issue, it can be extremely costly to the automaker to replace or fix it. Thus, perchance a software update can deal with it, the automaker is hopeful an OTA can do so. Does though the software merely mask something that genuinely needs to be replaced or fixed, and the band-aid is marginally mollifying the risk.

• Will an OTA fix one thing and yet cause or lead to some other problem?

It could be that an OTA software fix ultimately leads to some other problem that will emerge down-the-road, such as causing greater wear-and-tear on other parts of the car or have other unintended consequences.

Conclusion

When an OTA changes your car's infotainment system, any kind of software screw-up is relatively inconsequential. When the OTA is altering the core driving capabilities, the consequences can be tremendous.

OTA in one sense provides a low-cost and easy way to transmit changes across thousands upon thousands of cars, in nearly the blink of an eye, yet it can also as easily spread something that is amiss. Besides the automaker leveraging this handy logistics capability, hopefully responsibly, there is also the temptation for bad actors to use it to deploy untoward cyber-hacks. That box of chocolates might contain some foul-tasting candies or even potentially venomous ones.

CHAPTER 3
SURVEYS
AND
AI SELF-DRIVING CARS

CHAPTER 3

SURVEYS
AND
AI SELF-DRIVING CARS

There are numerous online surveys and phone-based polls being taken about whether or not the lay public is ready for the advent of driverless autonomous cars. Results released recently by a study conducted by the American Automobile Association (AAA) indicated that 71% of United States drivers said they would be afraid to ride in a self-driving car. If you extrapolate that 71% to the entire estimated number of licensed drivers in the U.S., it comes out to about 175,000,000 Americans with that qualm.

Some critics have bemoaned that those lay public are merely scaredy-cats, afraid of their own shadow, perhaps Luddites that oppose all new technology, and generally are unwashed and unversed in what is taking place with autonomous cars.

I'd say those 175,000,000 Americans are right to be cautious and skeptical for now, and furthermore, I wonder what the other 75,000,000 are thinking (more on this in a moment) if they don't have a healthy dose of doubt at this time.

In essence, I do not find those with uncertainties to be off-base.

We do not yet know whether a true Level 5 fully autonomous car can actually be devised and fielded.

The tryouts on our roadways today tend to involve semi-autonomous cars that require a licensed human driver to co-share the driving task. For those less-than Level 5 driverless cars that are at a Level 4, thankfully there is so far a back-up human driver, presumably ready to take over, though we've seen that this can be a somewhat false assumption per the Uber deadly crash into a pedestrian of last year (there are numerous risks when expecting a back-up human driver to leap to the rescue).

You have every right to be watching the driverless car emergence with an air of cautiousness. Some would argue that we are allowing these eager automakers and tech firms to make us all into experimental guinea pigs, placing self-driving cars onto our roadways and within grasp of our own human-driven cars and human walking pedestrians, and bicyclists, and motorcyclists, and dogs and cats that might run across the street. The at-times overboard fail-fast fail-often mantra of the tech world doesn't map too well when there are lives at stake.

The stance by the makers of autonomous cars is that they won't be able to make substantive progress unless their self-driving cars are on everyday roadways. The use of special closed tracks or proving grounds is considered insufficient, lacking in the variety and variability that a real-world set of streets and highways provides. The use of simulation is being generally pursued, though critics adamantly say it is not being given enough due, and furthermore that until bona fide simulation results are provided and verified, these POC (Proof Of Concept) efforts are dangerous and unwarranted.

More Surveys And More Grist For The Mill

In a study undertaken by J.D. Power and the NAMIC (National Association of Mutual Insurance Companies), released in Fall 2018, the online survey asked automobile insurance customers a series of questions about their opinions of driverless cars.

There were 15% that said there will never be a fully automated vehicle, which I disagree with since to suggest that there will never ever be such a thing is rather bold and seemingly indeed a Luddite-kind of perspective. I'm confident we will ultimately have a true Level 5 self-driving car, it's merely a matter of when.

What's equally somewhat curious is the indication in that same survey that 42% of the respondents said they would not ride in a fully automated vehicle, no matter how many years after such an autonomous car was fully available on the marketplace. That's nearly half saying that would never ride in one, no matter presumably how validated and safe it might be. A somewhat futuristic doubting viewpoint, I'd say.

Another facet involves a question about how safe does a driverless car need to be before you'd ride in one, of which 38% said they would not ride in one no matter the safety level (this echoes the roughly 42% that I just mentioned), and an additional 45% said they require a 100% safe or 0% error rate. It's not clear what they mean by this. I've repeatedly exhorted that the idea of zero fatalities has a zero chance of happening since inevitably there will be circumstances of autonomous cars getting into car incidents of one kind or another.

My logic for breaking the falsehood of zero fatalities is that no matter how astute a self-driving car might be made to work, if someone darts into the street and there's insufficient distance to come to a stop, the physics of the situation overtakes the matter and injuries or deaths can occur. In addition, we are going to have a mixture of human-driven cars and driverless cars for quite a while, since it won't be an overnight switchover to autonomous cars, and the interplay will, of course, produce some number of rear-enders, bumper bashers, and all-out car wrecks.

Question-Wording Makes A Big Difference

In a Pew Research Center study released in October 2017, over half of the survey respondents said they would not want to ride in a driverless car (reportedly 56% indicated said as such). The nature of the question implied that they were being asked if they would want to ride in a driverless car at that time, rather than speculating about the future. I think their doubtfulness makes sense, at that time and still at this time.

This finding though also highlights something quite important about these myriads of surveys and polls, namely the way in which questions are worded or the context of how they are asked can materially shape the respondent answers.

For example, I've ridden in numerous of the driverless cars being devised but did so with at least one or two back-up drivers present. Thus, if I was asked whether I would want to ride in a driverless car, well, if the question means doing so without any kind of added safety efforts, my answer is no, but if the question means under controlled settings, my answer is a maybe or yes (depending upon the setup).

I am a resolute proponent of trying to standardize on the wording of these surveys and polls, which will help cut down on confusion when each otherwise idiosyncratic set of questions is asked, out of which we subsequently get a deluge of seemingly disparate answers by the public.

It's not that the public is necessarily out-of-sorts (which could be), but often that the questions asked are highly variant across different studies and produce therefore variant responses. There is a draft 26-item questionnaire called the Autonomous Vehicle Acceptance Model (AVAM) that has promise for trying to arrive at some kind of standardized way to assess public perception about driverless cars.

Conclusion

Speaking of wording, I mentioned earlier that 71% of Americans were apparently afraid or fearful to ride in a driverless car. The word "fearful" unfortunately has a lot of baggage or connotations associated with it. If someone asks you if you are fearful of something, it pushes you perhaps into a corner, since fears are often associated with being unfounded. The 29% of Americans that weren't "fearful" might consist of many that are doubtful or cautious, and yet didn't want to seemingly be listed as fearing something.

In my case, I don't fear driverless cars in the sense of them being a kind of Frankenstein, and instead, view autonomous cars as something that will continue to take time to be appropriately readied for being useful and unaided by human hands. That's also why I've devoted much of my professional career toward trying to arrive at autonomous vehicles.

Being cautious and watchful is prudent, and compatible with wanting to advocate for an innovation that will have substantive transformational impacts on us all and how we live.

CHAPTER 4

TECH SPIES
AND
AI SELF-DRIVING CARS

CHAPTER 4

TECH SPIES

AND

AI SELF-DRIVING CARS

Foreign spying seems to have been in the news quite a bit recently. The Russian femme fatale who recently pleaded guilty for transgressions during the 2016 U.S. presidential election was sentenced to a year-and-a-half of prison time for her deeds. Her case was prominently featured and widely debated.

One needs to consider how many spying instances go under-the-radar and are not quite so well-publicized, especially in the more cloistered high-tech fields, particularly self-driving tech.

Earlier this year there was an FBI bust of a Chinese citizen working at Apple who was accused of stealing its "Project Titan" self-driving car secrets. Allegedly, he had been found with thousands of Apple's files and documents pertaining to the company's proprietary autonomous vehicle materials and was trying to take the secrets overseas. In July 2018 the FBI had captured a different man, Xiaolang Zhang, also a former Apple employee, who apparently absconded with 40GB of crucial data also containing Apple's self-driving car aspects.

Last month, Tesla accused a former engineer of grabbing over 300,000 files to apparently hand them over to Xiaopeng Motors. According to Tesla, within those files were key records and actual programming source code of its vaunted Autopilot system.

These cases might well be the tip of the iceberg in terms of spies or potential spies lurking within the inner chambers of the automakers and tech firms developing autonomous car technology.

It can be problematic for such entities to provide a welcoming and open development environment for the hotshot, high-tech AI developers that they need to do this work, yet at the same time clamp down on keeping the files and code from being stolen by someone on the team. Handcuffing your tech wizards with need-to-know restrictions, while at the same time wanting to have them collaborate across the board, well, it's a tough balance to achieve.

Without too much herculean effort, pretty much any member of these self-driving tech teams tomorrow walk out the door tomorrow with a treasure trove.

What would someone do with the autonomous car proprietary materials that could be pilfered?

The most obvious answer is to use them to enhance your own driverless car efforts. And as such, these materials are typically being secreted to other self-driving tech makers. Sometimes it's a foreign firm that's trying to jump into the autonomous car realm on-the-cheap. In other cases, it might be a domestic competitor that hopes to leap forward by leveraging the handiwork of others.

The entity seeking the stolen info might not necessarily need the materials to make progress on their own. Instead, they're perhaps more so interested in what the other self-driving tech maker is doing and has accomplished. The ill-gotten materials are a kind of a barometer, letting the thieving firm grasp how far behind, or maybe even ahead, they might be in their own efforts.

A rarer twist involves wanting to discover if someone else maybe ripped you off, having taken something secretly from your own self-driving tech and subsequently incorporating it into a competitor's system.

If so, this might be a sign of crucial leakage within your own team, and it could also give rise to possibly going after the other firm for Intellectual Property (IP) losses and damages.

Another possibility, which won't yet be known or fully revealed for a while, consists of bad actors that want to examine the self-driving tech for cyber-weaknesses that can be exploited. These could possibly be used as zero-day exploits, meaning that once the autonomous cars by that automaker or tech firm become prevalent on the roadways, the nefarious plotters might have the means to hack them.

What Is In The Treasure Box

There is a wide range of self-driving tech materials that could be pinched and usefully leveraged by someone else that knew what they had in-hand.

• Source Code

Programming source code would be the customary first-item to grab. The magical code has likely required gobs of hours of expensive AI developer labor to craft. Ironically, the code might be based on hardware particulars and other nuances that make it less useful than you might think since not all code is easily ported over to other self-driving car designs. You could have something interesting but not especially helpful for the larcenous firm.

• System Designs

Another possibly handy item to lift would be the underlying designs and specifications of the self-driving tech. If the taking firm were at the start of its efforts, the fundamental designs could be a huge boost to getting rapidly underway. On the other hand, if that firm has already progressed far beyond the design stage, it's not clear that having someone else's designs would be especially useful since it might require a do-over to exploit them to any substantive degree.

• Deep Learning Models

Most of the self-driving tech guts consist of large-scale Deep Learning models, usually embodied in multilayer Artificial Neural Networks (ANN). These are potentially as valuable or more so than the programming source code materials. The nature of the models and their weights and structure could be quite helpful as a rip-off. A downside here though for the unethical firm is that these models are continually being updated and all they would have is a snapshot-in-time version.

• Reams of Data

Deep Learning models need lots of data to get primed and be able to perform their complex pattern matching. As such, it would be useful to purloin the mountains of data being used to train the ANN's of an autonomous car. The contemptable firm would not necessarily then need to bear the effort and cost of collecting such data. One hitch would be whether the data comes with labels, without which there could be a lot of added work that otherwise the data doesn't quite so amiably possess.

Conclusion

Don't be surprised if we continue to hear about spies within the self-driving tech world as they get rooted out or make a misstep that gets them nabbed. There's big money to be made via the advent of driverless cars and some want to shorten their own paths to get there, including using ill-gotten goods. Keep your eyes open, and your secrets closed.

CHAPTER 5
ANXIETIES
AND
AI SELF-DRIVING CARS

CHAPTER 5

ANXIETIES AND
AI SELF-DRIVING CARS

Though most people tend to have occasional anxieties over their everyday stressful lives in this modern nonstop world, there are some that experience a deeper and more persistent kind of anxiety, typically referred to as an anxiety disorder. As a frequent conference speaker about autonomous cars, I've seen repeatedly a fraction of attendees that appear to be quite anxious or in some instances intensely fearful about the potential arrival of self-driving driverless cars.

For those that seem to be on the verge of this perhaps unusual or new pedigree of a specific disorder that fixates on autonomous vehicles, they often exhibit a pronounced sense of impending doom or danger, they are extremely agitated and animated when asking questions or making statements about the future as they see it, and have reported that they are losing sleep and experiencing other physical and mental manifestations due to their anxiousness.

Let's give this a name, *autonomophobia*, if you were, and hope that it doesn't materialize in any substantive way.

I'm going to put aside herein those with this kind of ailment that ascribe to the belief that the advent of driverless cars is really an overall evil-doer plot to place humans into some kind of AI bondage, which is a notable member in the raft of AI conspiracy theories that seem to be floating around these days.

Those oft-repeated AI conspiracy theories typically involve AI becoming sentient, gaining a kind of human spark and then super-intelligence and decide then of its own newly found free-will to wipe us all out, those pesky and annoying human life forms. I don't think this has any real chance of happening in our lifetimes and have questioned whether these doomsday scenarios are more plausible than the happy-face versions.

It would seem more practical to concentrate on the indubitably prudent kinds of worrisome concerns. Based on the various questions and comments that I've gotten from attendees and readers of my columns; I've boiled down the anxiousness concerns into a Top 5 list.

Top Five Angsts Of The Autonomophobia Disorder

I'll cover the Top 5 angsts, offering insights about what they consist of, and the rationale or irrational basis for each one of them.

Angst #1: Will they take away my driver's license forever?

Pundits for driverless cars seem to keep saying that it will be best to ban all human driving in order to allow for the presumed safer and more "thoughtful" self-driving autonomous cars. As such, the word is spreading that any humans with a driver's license will become extinct, no more human driving allowed, all for the betterment of mankind.

This seems over-the-top, at least for the foreseeable future. There are over 250 million conventional cars in the United States alone, and the notion that autonomous cars would come into existence and overnight cause that entire stock of inventory to switchover, well, it's just not sensible.

For many years, likely decades ahead, there will be a mixture of human-driven cars and self-driving cars. It would seem unimaginable that regulators could somehow ban all human driving right away, even if they thought it worthwhile, and the contentious outcry and battle over such a change would be bitter and long-lasting.

Bottom-line, your driver's license isn't going away due to autonomous cars, any time soon.

Angst #2: Will I no longer be able to own a car?

According to recent statistics, it appears that Millennials and Gen Z are tending toward being less enamored about car ownership, partially due to being raised into an era of relatively widespread ridesharing. In spite of that apparent trend, there are still many that want to own a car, and even the latest generation that is less excited about owning multiple cars has been aiming toward owning at least one car, rather than giving up entirely on car ownership.

In any case, pundits about autonomous cars tend to assert that driverless cars will be entirely owned by large corporations such as the automakers and presumably the largest ridesharing firms, all grabbing up those self-driving cars as part of a money-making ridesharing fleet. This might be partially the case, but it seems to ignore or fail to realize that there will be lots of individual car owners that will opt to rideshare their driverless cars, and in many cases mini-fleets will emerge by budding entrepreneurs.

At Tesla's Autonomy Investor Day, Elon Musk touted the notion that individual car owners would be able to list their cars onto a Tesla ridesharing network, allowing for the use of their (someday) Full Self-Driving (FSD) car to make money for them. Imagine that you use your driverless car to take you to work, and the rest of the workday it is making money for you, likewise doing so after it has dropped you home for bedtime.

Bottom-line: Yes, there will still be individual car ownership in a world of driverless cars.

Angst #3: What am I to do while inside a driverless car?

For some, the mysterious nature of a car that can seemingly drive itself is also wrapped into the enigma of what the car will be like on the inside. This induces some to assume that they might be trapped inside the driverless car, a prisoner of a soulless machine that is going to take them someplace, wherever the automation decides. The human becomes impotent and no longer in control.

Well, that's certainly not what is on-the-docket for autonomous cars right now. Automakers are designing an interior that will allow the human passengers to swivel around and enjoy the company of other humans riding in the self-driving car or be able to gently sleep while being whisked to the office. I'm not saying that one couldn't devise a more ominous interior, only that it seems unlikely that such an approach will be undertaken and nor tolerated.

Bottom-line: Being inside a driverless car should be a pleasant ridesharing-like experience (that's the hope).

Angst #4: Might I get hit by a driverless car?

I've stated many times that the notion of zero fatalities and zero injuries due to the advent of self-driving cars is not achievable, and at best it is a lofty goal, though a tainted goal that is misleading and setting expectations beyond reach. So, yes, you can get hit by a driverless car.

As a pedestrian, if you opt to leap in front of an autonomous car that is coming down the street, presumably doing the legal speed limit, yet you suddenly appear without sufficient indication, the physics of the car, even a vaunted self-driving car, will be such that you are going to get hit. Sorry, there is no magical flying carpet or invisible shield that's going to overt this (well, at least none that we know of today).

Also, in the mix of human-driven cars and driverless cars, there are bound to be fender benders, rear-end run-ins and all kinds of car accidents or incidents. You also need to include in your calculus the chances of an AI system error or a hardware failure or fault that can get the autonomous car into untoward traffic troubles, possibly leading to human injuries or deaths.

Bottom-line: Self-driving cars will account for some amount of human injuries and deaths, though the intention is that it will be less than the amount sustained in today's human driving world.

Angst #5: Will I lose my job as a result of driverless cars?

I do not wish to be the bearer of bad news, but if your livelihood is based on driving a car, meaning you get paid because you are a human driver, your days are numbered in that profession, though as mentioned it will be quite a while before we see a widespread advent of autonomous cars, thus, you have time to get ready for changing your career direction and can likely continue your work for the foreseeable future.

The odds are that a lot of people are not going to trust a driverless car, at first, and for a while, and those passengers will be seeking a human driver rather than using an autonomous car. Another factor will be where driverless cars are geographically most likely to be first put into play, primarily high population centers, otherwise the ridesharing cost-benefit probably won't be a solid ROI.

Bottom-line: For now, you'll likely be able to continue being a paid driver of a car, though this will become gradually lessened and hopefully over time you'll be able to reskill to some other paying task.

Conclusion

Notice that each of the Top 5 angsts has a kernel of truth to it, though at a deeper analysis they are not quite as bad as much of the media tends to portray them. For those with the emerging *autonomophobia*, the media that overplays the hand of autonomous cars transforming our society almost overnight are adding more fuel to their anxiety fire, unfortunately, and I trust that my comments might let them catch a night's sleep, at least for a while.

CHAPTER 6

ACHILLES HEEL
AND
AI SELF-DRIVING CARS

CHAPTER 6

ACHILLES HEEL

AND

AI SELF-DRIVING CAR

When you were a young child, you might have placed your hand near a stovetop that was hot or tried to grab the handle of a pot or pan that had been on the stove and instinctively snatched back your hand. Having felt the intense heat, your autonomic nervous system kicked-in to save you from a severe burn.

At a later age, you likely used conscious reasoning to anticipate that a stovetop can be extremely hot, or a handle of a boiling pot or pan can be scalding, and so you cognitively make a mindful decision to avoid touching those potentially third-degree burn producing artifacts.

There is a delicate balance and tight dance between what your instinctive reaction is, and what your mindful reasoning consists of, and at times they might even be at odds with each other.

I remember one time I saw a pan on a stove that was starting to ignite its contents, potentially leading to a deadly fire, and I quickly reasoned that the most expedient act was to grab the pan by the handle and get it off the stovetop, yet I risked burning my hand in doing so.

My instincts fought against my reasoning, namely that instinctively my hand did not want to grasp that scorching hot handle, but I did so anyway, averting a larger disaster.

When it comes to key aspects of driverless autonomous cars, the same kind of delicate balance and tight dance takes place between automated instinctive features and a kind of more elaborated AI reasoning of sorts, particularly when it comes to braking an in-motion self-driving car.

The recently filed Tesla crash lawsuit involving the death of a human driver in a Tesla Model X provides a case in point on this kind of matter.

You might recall the headline-making case last year of the Uber self-driving car incident that led to the unfortunate death of a pedestrian. In my initial analysis posted just shortly after the incident was reported in the media, I predicted that there might have been some systems-related confounding issues that might have led to the brakes not being applied in a timelier matter. When the NTSB report was released, my prediction was characterized as prescient since indeed there was a system-related braking aspect involved.

It turned out that the Uber self-driving car engineers had previously disabled the inherent Volvo emergency braking capability, generically often referred to as Automatic Emergency Braking (AEB).

Why would such a seemingly oddball and risk-heightening act have been undertaken? Because the self-driving car engineers had devised their own AI-led emergency braking system and were concerned that having essentially two kinds of braking systems in the driverless car would lead to erratic behavior.

Imagine you were helping a novice teenage driver learn to drive a car, and suppose the car was equipped with two sets of brakes, one for you as the front seat passenger coaching the teenager, and then the usual brakes accessed by the skittish novice driver.

At any time, either of you could potentially apply the brakes. If you ponder this for a moment, you realize that it can lead to a great deal of confusion, and possible calamity, since either of you might suddenly slam on the brakes, catching the other one off-guard.

There's an added twist from a systems perspective.

The Automatic Emergency Braking can be implemented as an essentially simplistic and almost instinctive approach, detecting what it believes is the presence of an object ahead and based on a quite-and-dirty calculation the AEB urgently applies the brakes if it guesses that the object is going to get struck by the car. Alternatively, the Automatic Emergency Braking can be a more "reasoned" capability, involving a more robust AI system that assesses a wide variety of factors and sensory data, trying to arrive at a more intricately derived decision about hitting the brakes.

The more instinctive kind of AEB tends to be a faster form of responsiveness, yet it can also lead to falsely applying the brakes when the situation might not truly warrant it. The AEB that involves more of an AI analytic approach tends to be more well-rounded but can chew-up precious time, and as such lose opportunistic time that might have been spent in the actual braking of the car.

As a human driver, you at times need to make the same kind of instantaneous decisions. There's a possum in the roadway, do you jam on the brakes and hope to stop before you slam into the animal, but meanwhile perhaps there are other cars behind you that will ram into your car, and so maybe it is "safer" to not reactively apply the brakes and instead proceed ahead. Instinct versus reasoning.

You can have both types of AEB's on a self-driving car, though it is somewhat akin to having two masters and analogous to the novice teenage driver having access to the brakes and simultaneously so does the watchful parent.

Should the AI robust version of AEB be able to override the more simplistic instinctive AEB version?

Should the instinctive version be able to invoke itself even if the AI elaborated capability one has not yet ascertained whether urgent braking is a valid action to be undertaken?

It can be a bit of a conundrum.

Tesla Crash Lawsuit And The Automatic Emergency Braking System

In the Tesla crash lawsuit that involved the death of the driver, Walter Huang, there is a claim that the "2017 Model X was designed, built, and introduced into the stream of commerce without having been equipped with an effective automatic emergency braking system." Furthermore, the claim asserts that "Notwithstanding the fact the Tesla Model X vehicle was marketed and sold as a state-of-the-art automobile, the vehicle was without safe and effective automatic emergency braking safety features that were operable on the date of this collision."

In my earlier posting about the lawsuit boon that I've predicted is going to emerge in the autonomous car realm, I had emphasized that one area of close scrutiny in such cases will be what the automaker did or did not do in terms of the design, building, and fielding of their driverless car features.

This will undoubtedly force to the surface a lot of the engineering choices being made about self-driving cars, which are essentially unknown to the public per se right now, taking place in the backrooms and development labs, and will be potentially revealed once these lawsuits play out.

Having been an expert witness, I can also predict that the question of what was feasible at the time of an incident will become paramount, including what other automakers and tech firms were placing into operation at the time, and how the maker of the driverless car abided by or diverged from what was considered "standard" practice.

Conclusion

There's another angle to keep in mind especially about crashes involving Level 2 and Level 3 semi-autonomous cars, which are considered co-sharing of the driving task with a human driver and are decidedly not a true Level 5 fully autonomous car, namely what the human driver knew or didn't know about the AEB, it's capabilities and status, and whether the human and the AEB worked at odds with each other.

Some Level 2 and Level 3 semi-autonomous cars even allow the human driver to turn-off the AEB, which might be sensible for a human driver that doesn't want an automated system to suddenly be making braking decisions. On the other hand, if the human driver has disabled the feature, perhaps their life or the lives of others might have been saved if the AEB had been activated.

You can bet that lawsuits will be considering this aspect of the co-sharing relationship, plus whether the automaker sufficiently informed the human driver about the risks in turning off the AEB or in allowing the AEB to be on. Some say it's darned if you do, darned if you don't kind of predicament.

We are entering into an era of semi-autonomous cars that portend a plethora of risks when you have a co-sharing relationship between a human driver and the automation, at times sadly leading to an indelicate dance and untoward out-of-balance results.

CHAPTER 7

KIDS ALONE

AND

AI SELF-DRIVING CARS

CHAPTER 7

KIDS ALONE

AND

AI SELF-DRIVING CARS

There's a lot of hand-wringing these days about letting your children be solo passengers in ridesharing cars run by the conventional ridesharing services.

Some parents say that they would never let their young offspring be alone, i.e., without a trusted adult passenger, when going in a ridesharing vehicle, and are horrified that other parents even consider this rather untoward notion to be conceivable.

Meanwhile, some parents indicate that when pressed for time and having no other viable choice, they hesitantly and reluctantly let their kids use a ridesharing service.

For those that use a ride-sharing service as a last resort to get their son or daughter to baseball practice after school or get to a piano recital, such parents try to protect themselves and their children as much as possible. They get the child to take a picture of the driver and depending upon the ridesharing service can track via a mobile app the progress of the vehicle during its journey, along with sometimes having the child activate their FaceTime app on their own smartphone and try to let the parent enjoin virtually for the ride.

It is assumed by such parents that the ridesharing driver would not take a chance to do something adverse, given that they could be presumably identified and eventually hunted down.

The major ridesharing services such as Uber and Lyft even have a rule that any passenger under the age of 18 must be accompanied by an adult. Enforcement is somewhat loose in that it is up to the driver to carry out the rule, and the only substantive penalty is the potential for being banned from further driving for that ridesharing service, assuming they get caught.

Generally, the kids and the parents aren't likely to tattle on the driver, plus the driver is making money, sometimes with an added tip, and thus it is hard to know how prevalent the practice is and how often the rules are being skirted (there are smaller ridesharing services that cater to children as passengers, typically encompassing a premium price).

Consider a different twist, how would you feel about your child or children riding alone in an autonomous car, one that has no human driver in it at all?

Ramifications Of Driverless Cars On Children As Solo Passengers

Let's first all agree that we'll make an assumption that the autonomous car is considered roadway safe. I mention this because any self-driving driverless car that you wouldn't consider safe enough for you to ride in, well, I assume you wouldn't consider having your precious children ride in it either. Thus, the question about letting your children ride alone in a driverless car would only arise once you are already convinced that the autonomous car being used is safe and sound.

If there was a driverless car that you trusted as being roadworthy, would you no longer hesitate about letting your child go solo?

One upside is that there is no longer a human driver in the car, which takes that element out of the equation, relieving you of the anxiety that a human ridesharing driver might be a bad person. Also, it is anticipated that self-driving cars will be equipped with cameras pointing inward, doing so for purposes of keeping passengers from getting unruly and destroying the interior of a ridesharing car, allowing them to be recorded or real-time monitored while on a journey.

Some believe that you'll be able to tap into those cameras on a live stream basis, allowing you to keep watch on your child, perhaps via your desktop computer at work, and can likely carry on a dialogue with your child. Advances in electronic communications such as 5G will potentially allow you to readily interact and discuss how their day is coming along, what homework they have for that night, and maybe a quick pep talk as they are on their way to an after-school performance of some kind.

Your child can check-in when they first get into the self-driving car, then interact with you during the ride, and check-out with you after exiting from the driverless car, once they have reached their destination.

All in all, this would seem like a boon for parents that cannot otherwise provide a lift for their children via a friend driving a car or by themselves trekking around their child.

It is seemingly a quite welcome arrangement that their child will be inside a presumably secured space and not prone to anyone else approaching them. The child can perhaps work on other tasks while in the autonomous car, or be entertained by online video clips or movies, and could get a bite to eat since it is anticipated that ridesharing services with driverless cars are likely to offer food and beverages as an add-on money-maker.

An added plus is that you might not be using a ridesharing service at all, and instead own the driverless car. In that case, you dispatch it to go pick up your child and either it stays nearby to the child after performing the driving task, or maybe comes to work and picks you up, whisking you to where your child was getting music lessons for the last hour or so, and the two of you them use the family autonomous car to head back home together.

Downsides Of Children Alone In A Driverless Car

Unfortunately, the world is not always so rosy. There are some significant downsides to consider when allowing your children to ride alone in an autonomous car.

Suppose the driverless car gets into a pickle of some kind, such as a human-driven car happens to rear-end the self-driving car. You've now got your child mired into a mess, and you aren't there to help. Imagine the potentially traumatic impact on the child, having to deal with the situation on their own.

Another possibility is that the self-driving car encounters a situation that involves the AI deciding to bring the driverless car to a halt, parking at the side of the road, doing so because of some internal system fault or maybe as a result of the roadway conditions seeming to be outside the realm of what the autonomous car can handle. You've now stranded your child in a car, maybe in the middle of nowhere, or maybe in the middle of the worst part of town.

Let's also consider the aspect of whether a child inside a driverless car is going to be allowed to get out, on their own, if they wish to do so. Do you want your kindergartener child to be able to tell the autonomous car that it should come to a stop at the ice cream shop at the corner, and the child opens the car door and gets out, wanting to quickly get a fun snack? I doubt you'd want your child to be able to readily exit from the driverless car.

You might say that the driverless car should keep the child locked inside the car, no matter what the child says or does. But this could be wrong in situations whereby the child might need to urgently get out of the self-driving car due to a bona fide emergency.

Some autonomous cars might be outfitted with internal LED displays that indicate the status of the driverless car, being able to let a passenger know when the system or the car might be amiss and aiming to soon halt, but for children such displays or audio warnings could be confusing or scary, and of not much help.

It is also likely that automakers will include an OnStar-like capability of being able to have a remote agent that can talk with the passengers of the driverless car, which might sooth the nerves of a child when a self-driving car is having difficulties, though the remote agent isn't actually there in the automobile with the child and unable to truly do much other than try to calm an otherwise possibly panic stricken youngster.

Conclusion

With today's ridesharing services, when there is a child riding solo, in theory the human driver would hopefully exercise helpful or supportive judgment about dealing with situations if the car gets into a fender bender or if the child suddenly takes ill. This is a trade-off against the other side of the coin that the human driver might be a bad person and do something untoward.

In the case of an autonomous car, the elimination of the human driver seems to solve the untoward potential, but at the same time introduces new challenges when there is no adult whatsoever present in the moving car.

I've predicted that there might be a new kind of role that emerges, a kind of autonomous car chaperone or nanny, a trusted adult that goes along for the ride to help support solo-riding children.

Since the car is a driverless car, this person doesn't need to know how to drive and has nothing to do with the driving per se, instead they are presumably trained for and vetted as someone that can reliably interact with children. Ridesharing services are bound to offer this as an added service, for an extra cost or as an added incentive for you to use their driverless cars, along with other entities that might provide such chaperones akin to hiring a tutor for your kids.

As you can see, even with autonomous cars, there's no free lunch and the downsides of letting children ride solo shift in key respects and the driverless car is not necessarily a flawless panacea for how to get your kids from here to there.

CHAPTER 8

INFRASTRUCTURE

AND

AI SELF-DRIVING CARS

CHAPTER 8

INFRASTRUCTURE

AND

AI SELF-DRIVING CARS

There are emerging discussions that perhaps Congress and the White House might agree to a rather significant spend on America's infrastructure. Some say it could be on the order of $2 trillion potentially allocated. Whether or not you favor such an expenditure, most would likely agree that our infrastructure does seem to be progressively crumbling, as evidenced by everything from dams that break without apparent warning to a plethora of tire-bashing potholes permeating our roadways from coast-to-coast.

According to the most recent Report Card on our infrastructure by the American Society of Civil Engineers (ASCE), we all need to be seemingly ashamed of what we've allowed our country to become since the United States infrastructure earned a paltry and embarrassing D+ grade.

Just like a report card at school that covers various areas such as how you did in literature, math, history, and the like, the ASCE grades the infrastructure in sixteen notable categories.

Sadly, we got a C+ for our bridges, ports, and waste handling, and primarily D's for the rest of the categories, including a solid D for our roads and a D- for transit. Ouch, seems like we need to be kept after-school for some remedial work.

Meanwhile, if the proposed spending of perhaps $2 trillion dollars catches your breath, you'd better sit down, because the ASCE claims that we actually need to spend $4.5 trillion, doing so by the year 2025. You might consider the $2 trillion proposal a kind of part-way deposit and investment, which can be a starter, but it needs to be presumably amplified quite a bit over the next five years or so.

Without these investments, it is predicted that our infrastructure will continue to degrade, fall apart, likely causing lives to be lost, and lead to a slew of calamities that will leave us all shaken and regretful that we didn't take action beforehand to avoid the onslaught of our own infrastructure injuring and killing us.

In the midst of all this, one question that needs to be asked involves this: *What about autonomous driverless cars?*

Self-Driving Driverless Cars And The Infrastructure

Many pundits focused on the spending for America's infrastructure are at times not taking into account the hoped-for emergence of autonomous cars. Regrettably and inexcusably so.

I assert that the infrastructure investments being contemplated need to ensure that there is a piece-of-the-pie for self-driving driverless cars.

At least make sure that the autonomous car topic gets onto the table of deliberations about where and in what ways to maintain, fix, upgrade, and enhance our infrastructure, particularly the transportation side of things.

Anyone not including driverless car aspects into any infrastructure considerations would be short-sighted in their views. It would ultimately be a gut-wrenching omission that after-the-fact would be realized as having been a glaring and disconcerting loss of opportunity, potentially delaying the advent of driverless cars or inadvertently raising the cost and effort to bring them to fruition.

That being said, there are overly rabid fans of self-driving cars that should be cautioned about unreasonably asking that the entire country be retrofitted to somehow accommodate autonomous cars. I am decidedly not a devotee of those that think our transportation approach must be radically altered simply to enable driverless cars to succeed.

As an example, some idealists want to convert all of our roadways into driverless-only streets and highways, banning any human driving, taking away people's drivers licenses, and otherwise becoming their version of a Utopian AI-driven world. This flies in the face of today's reality.

Face it, there are over 250 million conventional cars in the United States and those aren't going to be mothballed overnight, nor will driverless cars appear overnight and become pervasive instantaneously. Bottom-line is that we are going to have both human-driven cars and self-driving cars mixing together on our roadways for a long time to come. You can dream about a future that might be many decades away, maybe, but let's deal with transportation elements now that can aid the foreseeable and progressive advent of autonomous cars.

Traditional And Newer Digital Infrastructure Elements

It is instructive to divide the car-oriented infrastructure elements into two groupings, consisting of the traditional aspects and the newer digital aspects. Each of those groupings can be directly helpful to the emergence of driverless cars. They are not necessarily mutually exclusive or working at odds with each other.

For example, let's consider potholes. We all hate them, except for maybe tire stores and auto repair shops.

Fixing our nation's potholes would be considered a traditionalist infrastructure kind of action. Getting rid of those teeth-jarring and axel-bending potholes is good for conventional cars, and fortunately turns out to be good for self-driving cars too (there's no magic imbued in autonomous cars that allows them to hover above those dastardly potholes and avoid them, at least not yet). You might say that dealing with potholes is a twofer.

There are some traditionalist aspects that can be amped-up to more favorably aid driverless cars.

Ponder for a moment lane markings.

The lane markings on the roads that indicate where a lane boundary is, those are obviously helpful to human drivers, and likewise tend to be used by autonomous cars, based on the camera sensory devices and the use of AI to interpret the visual scene ahead. One approach involves using conventional paints and dumb-markers to freshen and highlight the roadway path, while an enhanced approach would use specialized paints and smart-markers, providing a potent digital enablement.

What do I mean by digital enablement?

The driverless car could use the cameras to visually process what it sees, and in addition, would be able to pick-up electronic communications that the digitally enabled street-oriented capabilities might provide. Human drivers might not be able to leverage the digital beaconing, yet they still would be able to better see the lanes due to the refreshing of the markings, and once again you are getting a kind of twofer.

There are digital infrastructure add-ons that would be perhaps less valued by human drivers, including for example the use of edge computing devices, placed along highways and roadways, enabling capabilities for V2V (vehicle-to-vehicle), V2I (vehicle-to-infrastructure), V2P (vehicle-to-pedestrian), and other V2X (X meaning all-encompassing) connecting with self-driving cars. These kinds of electronic communications would contribute toward the safety of driverless cars, along with their efficient and effective usage.

Interestingly, human drivers could indeed benefit from those otherwise automation-focused improvements. A human driver could receive electronic alerts and communiques to their semi-autonomous car, of which the human might utilize during the driving task. Let's though be careful about how this might be implemented, since the result could be a barrage of distractions that cause the human driver to get into car accidents, producing adverse undesirable consequences rather than being helpful.

Another looming question is the role of Electrical Vehicles (EV) and our transportation infrastructure.

Generally, autonomous cars are likely to be EV-based, partially due to the enormous electrical cravings of the onboard sensors and computers. A driverless car does not need to be an EV, but it makes life easier since an EV is built with electrical power as a core capability that dovetails into the needs of self-driving cars.

As such, one wonders, should our country-wide infrastructure be outfitted with charging stations, doing so to accommodate the assumed growth in EV usage. Right now, the EV adoption has been sluggish partly due to the consumer complaint that unlike having gasoline stations on every corner, trying to find a place to charge your EV is currently problematic. If the U.S. infrastructure made an investment in charging stations, this qualm might be lessened or overcome.

It's another potential twofer, encouraging people to switch over to EVs, and simultaneously potentially benefiting the emergence of autonomous cars that are EV-based.

Conclusion

Per my earlier remark, whether you believe in spending on infrastructure or not, and whether the potential of $2 trillion dollars makes your eyes bug out, nonetheless I assert that whatever we all opt to do about our crumbling infrastructure, let's make sure to provide attention to autonomous cars, especially since there are many prudent ways to get a twofer out of our hefty infrastructure investments.

CHAPTER 9

DISTRACTED DRIVING

AND

AI SELF-DRIVING CARS

CHAPTER 9

DISTRACTED DRIVING

AND

AI SELF-DRIVING CARS

All it takes is a brief moment of distraction and your world can change radically for the worse.

When driving a car, a split-second difference can determine whether you ram into that car ahead of you, or maybe sideswipe an innocent bike rider, or hit the guardrail at the edge of the lane you are in. Any of those horrific moments can produce injuries or deaths for the driver and other unlucky people that perchance got snarled into the dreadful mess.

In spite of this reality, most drivers readily allow themselves to become distracted or actually take overt actions that indisputably are distracting and for which the driver knew or certainly should have known that it would be.

In the estimated 37,000 fatalities per year that occur in the United States due to car accidents, statistics by the NHTSA suggest that perhaps 16% were due to distracted driving aspects. Harshly stated, that is about 6,000 human beings killed in the U.S. each year as a result of a distracted driver (or, about 15 people per day).

Meanwhile, there are about 6.3 million car crashes in the U.S. each year, which if we assume that maybe 16% of those are as a result of a distracted driver, this means that over 1 million car crashes annually or approximately 2,700 each day are taking place by the hands of a distracted driver.

You could say it is an epidemic or plague of distracted drivers.

Some hope that once we have autonomous cars, those days of death and injury from distracted human drivers will be behind us. Keep in mind though that this presumably would only occur once we had ditched all conventional human-driven cars and had only driverless cars on our roadways. Let's be serious and acknowledge that won't happen for many decades from now, if ever (there are 250 million conventional human-driven cars in America today, and they will last a long time).

On the path to driverless cars, distracted driving is going to worsen, ironically perhaps, and we are bound to experience even more injuries and deaths exacerbated by the journey to self-driving autonomous cars.

How Distracted Driving Arises

Let's start this examination of distracted driving by analyzing how it arises.

You could assert that distracted driving is nothing new.

For those of you that have been driving prior to the prevalence of GPS systems, you certainly must recall those days of unfolding a paper-based map and having it draped all across your lap and the dashboard. That was distracting, and many movies and TV shows often made light of the matter, highlighting the driver swerving and trying to keep their eyes on the road while also scrutinizing the map.

By-and-large there are now GPS systems either built into the car console or that drivers use via their smartphones. This might have alleviated the folding and unfolding of a paper-based map, but it still involves a form of distraction, typically involving glancing at the screen to see what the directions indicate.

Sure, most GPS systems also have turn-by-turn voice instructions, reducing the amount of eye time devoted to looking at a screen, yet you'd be hard pressed to claim that people never look at the GPS screen. They do.

We all might be somewhat sympathetic to distracted driving that involves an act that could be described as integral to driving the car, such as inspecting a map, though not much sympathy since it is a deadly choice, while those that are distracted by other comportments of discretionary actions are really just inexcusable. Eating a burger, not particularly essential to the driving task. Putting on your make-up or getting that early morning shave completed, it's not helping you with the steering wheel or the brake pedal.

Some point to today's society and suggest that the ease of drive-thru eateries for a quick meal while driving is a grand temptress for distracted driving. The advent of smartphones and the intense desire to keep-up with your emails is another inducement to distracted driving. Worse of all, some say, involves texting while driving. You convince yourself that a few pecks on your virtual keyboard of your smartphone could not possibly impact your driving efforts, plus the FOMO (Fear Of Missing Out) is so powerful of a primitive urge that it overrides your more deliberate realization of the magnitude associated with properly performing the driving task in an unfettered way.

Intexticide is being added to our lexicon as a mash-up by some as suggesting that texting while driving is a form of driving-induced suicide (a variant of the more "conventional" texticide).

Semi-Autonomous Cars Are Going To Amp-Up Distracted Driving

We can all agree that if there were no human drivers, there would not be any human distracted drivers (since we're agreeing in this assumed use case that there aren't any human drivers), and thus the belief logically follows that if we had only driverless cars there would no longer be distracted driving. My only hesitation with this notion is that in theory an autonomous car could also become "distracted" while driving, not due to eating a hamburger, but due to a potential overloading of sensory activity that could confound the AI system, though let's set that aside for the moment as another matter for another day.

How can we seek to achieve autonomous cars?

Two major avenues:

• We could make semi-autonomous cars that require a human driver, and gradually extend the semi-autonomous capabilities over time, incrementally, year after year, until presumably the vehicle reaches a point of autonomy, no longer needing the human driver to co-share the driving task.

• Or, an alternative approach involves skipping past semi-autonomous cars and producing purely and truly self-driving cars (known as Level 5 autonomous cars).

Most of the automakers are pursuing the semi-autonomous car route, as per the emergence of Level 3 cars. These Level 3 cars have a slew of additional bells and whistle augmenting the ADAS (Advanced Driver-Assistance Systems), trying to make these vehicles become more astute for the driving task. Nonetheless, a human driver is still needed and expected to be actively engaged in the driving effort.

Here's how the pain is going to get worse. Some or more likely many human drivers will become lulled into complacency and believe that they no longer need to concentrate on the driving task. At their own choosing, they will not just text, not just shave, not just do emails, they will decide to watch full-length video movies and get mentally immersed in other far reaching cognitive contortions that have nothing to do with the driving whatsoever.

Even if the automaker tells them they need to stay attune to driving, the temptation is now twofold, their false belief that they don't need to remain engaged in driving, coupled with their desire to do something else (maybe even closing their eyes and catching a nap). Notably, their distracted driving is not merely about themselves, which some immediately claim, since if their semi-autonomous car goes awry, it can injure or kill others, those in nearby cars or pedestrians or motorcyclists, etc.

Conclusion

I'll add another twist that few are yet considering.

Suppose we equip semi-autonomous cars with monitoring features that detect the distracted driver and alert them to get back into the game. This seems to solve the distracted driver problem. Not entirely, though, since another part of the equation is the complexity of the semi-autonomous systems and how they will be communicating with the human driver.

Think of it this way. Pretend that you had a front seat passenger that had a second set of driving controls in your car. You and your passenger are co-sharing the driving task. When your passenger is going to make a left turn, they tell you that a left turn is imminent. They also tell you they are leaning on the brakes to make the turn. They also tell you that there's a pedestrian crossing the street and so it will be a wider swing of a turn. And so on.

You can become "distracted" by efforts integral to the driving task, really integral, and need to balance those while also deciding what you will be doing during the driving effort. Two heads are often said to be better than one, but not necessarily when you are trying to drive a car. Advances in semi-autonomous cars have the potential for a double whammy on distracted driving.

CHAPTER 10

HUMAN DRIVERS

AND

AI SELF-DRIVING CARS

CHAPTER 10

HUMAN DRIVERS

AND

AI SELF-DRIVING CARS

For those automakers and tech firms aiming to produce a truly autonomous car, considered a Level 5, they are using our public roadways as a means to tryout their experimental driverless cars, doing so to augment efforts undertaken on special closed-track proving grounds and as also based on various computer-based simulated driving trials.

There is controversy underlying the use of public roadways for this testing and exploration effort, partially due to the chances that if something goes awry the result could harm humans that might be near to the possibly wayward vehicle.

You can usually recognize one of these self-driving cars by the sensory equipment lashed to the top of the car, such as the bulbous-like oft-used LIDAR (a sensing device that combines the use of light with radar), and sometimes too the exterior of the car is emblazoned with signage indicating the automaker or tech company that is supporting the autonomous car development.

If you happen to live or drive in an area that has such vehicles, you would likely at first be rather tickled to see a driverless car as it sashays down the street, and apt to gape at it, perhaps even video recording its presence on your smartphone as though this was a rare sighting, akin to seeing a horse galloping along on asphalt or a surprise appearance of a wayward goose on a hectic roadway.

In the Silicon Valley area, I see these driverless cars quite frequently and have grown rather accustomed to seeing them.

Here's a rather inconvenient truth, human drivers and these AI driverless cars tend to not mix well together. In many respects, they are like oil and water.

How Human Drivers React When Near To Driverless Cars

You can usually divide those that observe an autonomous car into two categories.

There's the first-timers, typically gaping at a driverless car, and then there are the overly-seasoned underwhelmed, the who-cares "hackneyed" that have seen these self-driving cars over and again.

The first-timers consist of people that have not seen a driverless car with their own eyes, other than in newspaper pictures and online videos, and they are usually taken by surprise to witness an actual autonomous car. It brings a sense of awe to them. The future is right there, in front of them, making its way past their local neighborhood shops and peaceful homes, imbuing amazement and a kind of spiritual moment in which science fiction seems to nearly be real.

When I say this, keep in mind that these driverless cars nearly always have a human back-up driver in the vehicle, and therefore the car is not entirely "driverless" per se, meaning that you can still spot the human inside the car, and at times there are two back-up drivers present (one that is supposed to be the primary back-up, and the second an engineer serving as a secondary back-up and aiming to keep the primary alert and awake). Thus, I'd dare say it could be even more shocking to some when they see an autonomous car without any human inside (today this happens mainly on a closed track).

Let's consider the reactions of human drivers when they spot a driverless car, the reaction of which tends to be based on whether the human driver is a first-timer witness (not having seen an autonomous car in action before) or whether the human is of the hackneyed type (been near to driverless cars with some frequency).

First-Timers Coming Upon A Driverless Car

The human driver that is a first-timer witness will often give the autonomous car a huge berth, akin to the distance you might allocate if you saw a teenage novice driver in one of those cars marked as a driving school instructional vehicle.

We all know that teenage novice drivers can be potentially unpredictable. As novice drivers, they haven't yet figured out how to use the brakes appropriately, nor when to steer clear of emerging traffic difficulties, and so on. Similar to the desire to not get entangled with a teenage novice driver, the first-time human drivers that come upon a driverless car are usually skittish around the self-driving car, giving it whatever right-of-way that it might need, even when unwarranted.

You might be tempted to assume that this is a healthy reaction and wise to give the autonomous car extra room and not try to pressure it or make it feel boxed-in. Ironically, this is actually not so good for the self-driving car.

Why? Because most of the time the driverless car is trying to use Machine Learning to figure out how to best drive on our roadways ("learning" to drive a car by whatever occurs while actually driving a car). Imagine a teenage driver that only learned how to drive when everyone else avoided their car, and then assume the teenager was later thrust into a situation whereby nobody knew that a teenage novice was driving a car in their midst – the result could be cataclysmic.

That being said, I certainly don't blame you for being highly suspicious of the driverless car and wanting to keep your distance from it. You have every right to assume that the self-driving car might make a misstep, and furthermore that the human back-up driver might not catch the matter in-time (assuming there is a back-up driver present).

Better to be safe than sorry, it's a fair way to react.

Seasoned Hackneyed Drivers Near To Autonomous Cars

Now consider the seasoned human drivers that have come upon autonomous cars numerous times. This does indeed happen in particular areas of Silicon Valley, due to the driverless car tryouts being concentrated in carefully chosen neighborhoods and locales, thus, you can readily see these vehicles meandering back-and-forth routinely. It can become numbing and so humdrum that you barely even notice that one of them is nearby you.

The hackneyed human drivers have come to realize that most of the driverless cars are like driving next to a simpleton, involving the AI being at times overly cautious, uptight, spasmodic, and occasionally stubborn as a mule. Currently, most autonomous cars are setup to abide by the speed limit, religiously, and otherwise do not drive in a fluid manner that a human driver would. This can gum up traffic, becoming an irritant and a form of exasperation for savvy human drivers.

For those weathered human drivers that have endured being around today's autonomous cars, they have also discovered that they can outrun and outfox the driverless car. Why wait behind the slowpoke self-driving car when you can skip around it, and it won't seemingly care. Why not proceed to cut-off the driverless car so that you can make a turn sooner, and therefore not need to get stuck waiting for the stilted AI to get the self-driving car to agonizingly slowly make that same turn.

Conclusion

The existing crop of driverless cars are a minority in that there are few of them as yet on our streets. It would be like having teenage novice drivers from time-to-time getting their driving lessons in your area. If the capabilities of these autonomous cars aren't radically improved, and if more of them are brought onto our roadways, we'll be mixing together oil and water. They don't mix very well.

Imagine your entire neighborhood flooded daily and hourly with teenage novice drivers weaving throughout in their learning-to-drive mechanizations. Scary. Note though that at least a teenager is exercising some modicum of human reasoning, a relief in many ways over the bleaker AI autonomy capabilities.

Should we ban driverless cars from public roadways until they are better proven to be more capable drivers? Some say adamantly yes, while others say that the difficulties and risks are worth what might be gained.

In a rather mind-bending twist, there is a contingent that says we should ban all human drivers from our roadways, which would presumably allow the autonomous cars to avoid dealing with crazy human driving foibles. That right now is a non-starter notion and an entirely impractical proposition.

For the moment, apparently it will be oil and water. Keep this in mind when you are driving home tonight, just in case you encounter an autonomous car.

.

CHAPTER 11

ANTI-LIDAR STANCE

AND

AI SELF-DRIVING CARS

CHAPTER 11

ANTI-LIDAR STANCE

AND

AI SELF-DRIVING CARS

Readers have asked me to augment my remarks about Tesla's Investor Autonomy Day, in which I had indicated Elon Musk decidedly and antagonistically threw down the gauntlet to bolster his stance questioning the use of LIDAR (a type of sensor that uses light and radar). In fact, he hurled the gauntlet right into the face of the rest of the autonomous car industry and those that make the devices.

In short, Musk has unequivocally become the defacto head of camp anti-LIDAR.

Keep in mind that nearly all other driverless car makers are incorporating the use of LIDAR in their vision systems. Furthermore, tech companies that already make the sensors or that are developing LIDAR units have blossomed recently, amounting to over 80 such innovative firms (per SAE's Automotive Engineering magazineindication), and have unabashedly attracted VC/PE monies readily.

You've got one voracious trumpeter bleating to the hills that LIDAR is verboten, taking an overt and highly visible anti-LIDAR posture, and then just about everyone else embracing LIDAR for autonomous cars. And though sometimes a contrarian can be right, they are often also as likely to be wrong, maybe more so.

It's now become an undeniably sizable gamble by Musk and a humongous bet that could ultimately undermine Tesla's chances of survival, which I'll explain herein.

How Did We Get Here

Prior to his extremely vitriolic anti-LIDAR proclamation, Musk had generally been a bit more muted about his position (muted is a relative term).

Let's go back in time to eons ago, early 2018, perhaps considered many dog-years long now past though only about one year ago, and realize that he had argued that LIDAR was overly expensive, bulky, and he viewed it as a kind of crutch, though he also had conceded: "Perhaps I am wrong, and I will look like a fool. But I am quite certain that I am not."

On April 22, 2019 (Tesla's Investor Autonomy Day), the world seemed to be quite a different place, in terms of Elon's opinion about LIDAR, becoming shall we say less-reserved and more adamant, here's what he proclaimed: "LIDAR is a fool's errand. Anyone relying on LIDAR is doomed. Doomed!"

Mildly, one could assert that he has opted to double-down on his bet.

Earlier, he had hedged just a tad, offering the possibility that LIDAR might be of value. Now, he's become the anti-LIDAR proclaimer, using his loudspeaker to declare LIDAR as null-and-void.

Worse still, his remarks assert that others using or investing in LIDAR for autonomous cars are foolhardy in doing so, presumably wasting money, time, energy, and their spirits on a (he suggests) condemned technology.

Musk often takes the air out of a room, but this one was especially rough, leaving others in the autonomous car industry to gasp, though given the oft-used hyperbole arising from Tesla and Musk, it wasn't a surprise for those already used to his at-times outrageous (bold?) decrees.

What Is LIDAR

To clarify, LIDAR has been that bulbous-like cap that you've undoubtedly seen sitting on the top of autonomous cars.

It shoots out light beams, the light beams bounce off of nearby objects, the returning beams are then collected up by the LIDAR unit. This is akin to radar and allows for the measurement of distances to objects, within the range of the LIDAR device being used. The AI system of the autonomous car then interprets the collected data to try and figure out what objects are nearby, along with the shapes of the objects, their amount of movement over time, their direction or heading, and so on.

When most of the autonomous car makers got started with devising driverless cars, they tended to include LIDAR units into their overall AI system for the cars. Musk is right about the notion that the LIDAR units were earlier costly and bulky, but that's somewhat like living in the past since advances in tech have brought the costs remarkably down and the sizes are remarkably smaller too. In fact, so much so that many of the driverless cars now have multiple LIDAR units and you can barely notice them.

It is much harder these days to bolster the anti-LIDAR argument by the claims of the bulkiness of LIDAR units and also of the costliness of LIDAR units.

Doing so is one of those waving of the hands kind of arguments that don't particularly hold water anymore, though some continue to cling to it anyway. Let's set aside that part of the argument as worn torn and increasingly being less relevant.

Instead, consider an ongoing technical argument underway in the halls of autonomous car makers and researchers about the merits of LIDAR versus cameras, and the anti-LIDAR camp that wants to assert that cameras are sufficient by themselves and that LIDAR is not needed.

In essence, some say that since humans use only their eyes when driving, and cannot shoot light beams from their heads, maybe this implies that cameras-alone are sufficient and that LIDAR is unnecessary (the classic retort is that humans only have legs, so presumably cars should have legs rather than wheels, pointing out that solely mimicking human features is not really much of a valid argument per se).

What immediately undercuts the key point of cameras-only is that nearly everyone seems to agree to-date that using radar is an essential partner to the use of cameras. Even Musk allowed that this was the case for Tesla and indeed Tesla cars are outfitted with radar. If that's the case, then it becomes a debate about presumably whether to use conventional radar versus LIDAR, since the door has already been opened to agreeing that radar of some kind is warranted, rather than being preoccupied with the LIDAR versus cameras dialogue.

Taking us more deeply into the acrimonious debate, the usual reply by the cameras-only camp is that conventional radar is merely a temporary bridge and once the cameras are good enough, apparently the radar will not be needed or will be considered a mere convenience of availability. They often toss into their points the notion that radar is less expensive than LIDAR and less bulky, but as I've already alluded to herein, those offhand comments won't stand the test of time.

Why This Anti-LIDAR Is A Hefty Gamble

I assert that these back-and-forth arguments are missing some rather fateful aspects that have an even greater weight on the future of autonomous cars and especially those driverless cars in the anti-LIDAR encampment.

When an autonomous car gets into an accident, which mark my words will happen, you can be further assured that lawsuits will be filed. I've previously described that one of the key elements of such lawsuits will be what did the autonomous car maker do as part of the design, building, and fielding of their self-driving car, and particularly how did they seek to ensure safety and reliability.

For Tesla, if pressed by a lawsuit, they will need to defend in court their decision to not use LIDAR. As you can imagine, Tesla will be on rather shaky ground if it is shown that essentially all other autonomous cars are using LIDAR. The burden to explain and justify the lack of LIDAR on Tesla's is going to be mighty steep.

And, more damming, I've pointed out many times that Musk's assertion that the cost of LIDAR is "expensive" will put Tesla into even murkier waters, bringing to the forefront a cost-related issue.

Assuming that people have died in the car accident, the question will be pointedly what was the cost of a LIDAR unit at the time and its incorporation into a driverless car, versus the cost of the human lives that were lost. Traditional automakers know by the school-of-hard-knocks that juries and judges take a dim view on matters involving cutting corners that can be attributed to a less safe or less reliable vehicle (recall the famous Pinto case and the clamor over the cost of safety versus the cost of human lives).

The Tesla position would presumably be that the addition of LIDAR would not have materially avoided the car accident and loss of lives, but this is going to be tough to showcase since in theory any use of LIDAR is going to incrementally improve the safety odds, assuming it is used wisely, and so it's another part of the uphill climb by Tesla to avoid getting summarily dinged for their lack of LIDAR.

They also cannot make the argument that they did not know about LIDAR or were somehow unaware of it, which is quite obviously not the case, including that their self-offered anti-LIDAR rhetoric acting as their own admission that they knew about LIDAR and made a deliberate decision to intentionally exclude it.

Conclusion

Even if Musk were tomorrow to change his mind and opt to switchover to the LIDAR camp, Tesla has repeatedly stated that Tesla cars already have the necessary hardware for autonomous capabilities. This implies that Tesla would be on-the-hook to outfit Tesla's with LIDAR, after-the-fact, retrofitting them all, a very costly and logistically unimaginable ordeal, if they had an epiphany and utter change-of-heart about LIDAR.

In brief, Tesla is now painted into a tight corner.

They cannot readily climb out of the anti-LIDAR mode into the LIDAR adopters group, and when it comes time to defend themselves in court, it is going to be easier to explain to juries and judges that Tesla omitted something that everyone else is using and for which it might well have contributed to avoiding the accident and deaths, in comparison to Tesla trying to argue that they did just fine without LIDAR (plus, mired in explaining why they scrimped presumably on cost, implying some kind of cost-versus-human-lives calculus was involved).

If that kind of case occurs and goes against Tesla, or even if it merely raises awkward questions about the safety of Tesla cars in-absence of having LIDAR, it could stir public opinion on driverless cars that are lacking in LIDAR and even spark regulators into action.

Anyway, it's quite an interesting bet that Musk and Tesla are making and the roll of the dice is already underway.

CHAPTER 12

AUTOPILOT TEAM

AND

AI SELF-DRIVING CARS

CHAPTER 12

AUTOPILOT TEAM

AND

AI SELF-DRIVING CARS

Being a leader is hard. In my book about business leadership and CEOs, I point out that CEO's are often dogmatic and strive to portray an image to their teams that suggests they are clear cut in what is expected and adamant in exuding unflinching confidence, doing so to win over any waffling or dissent that might be brewing inside the firm.

Ironically, this same kind of self-assuredness can be a weakness for the CEO because they tend to assume that they are clearly part of the solution and yet never part of the problem. At times, a CEO can undermine his or her own aspirations and make problems worse in the organization by deciding to step in directly and act precipitously.

One of the tools used most often by a CEO consists of the seeming cure-all act of an organizational restructuring. If things aren't going well at the company, find the part of the firm that's presumably underperforming, and move the people around to find a better fit that will bring the desired outputs, along with cutting out those that aren't conducive and perhaps adding some fresh meat into the mix.

There have been many instances of CEO's telegraphing to Wall Street that the old ways aren't going to be tolerated and a restructure is going to turn the company around.

This has the appearance of righteous action and being decisive, yet in-the-end it could be that the restructuring doesn't make things better, possibly even makes things worse, and can regrettably be akin to simply moving the chairs around on the deck of the Titanic (it's not going to keep the ship afloat).

So, whenever you hear about a CEO that's undertaken a restructuring, it is prudent to consider whether the restructuring will lead to a happy face of grand improvements, or whether it might produce a sad face and worsen whatever downhill slide was already underway (note: you can usually assume there was some kind of downhill slide, since otherwise why undergo the typical angst and disquieting contortions involved in undertaking a restructuring).

The double whammy part can be that the CEO decides to become more involved in the part of the firm that's being restructured. It's one thing to have a restructuring carried out and then for the CEO to keep tabs on how things are faring, while another more invasive approach involves putting yourself, the CEO, essentially into the functional area and deciding it's time to roll up your sleeves and be more engaged in the function.

There are trade-offs of this notion, including a presumed benefit that the CEO is now closer to the action, but it can also mean that their already limited time and availability is being splintered further, perhaps distracting the CEO from other even more important executive actions needed for the firm.

You'll see in a moment the importance of my offering this quick preamble about leadership, restructuring, and the like.

Restructuring Of The Tesla Autopilot Team

A recent report in the media indicates that Elon Musk has opted to restructure the Tesla Autopilot team, which is at the core of the autonomous car ambitions there, and he supposedly did so within a few weeks after the Tesla Investor Autonomy Day took place (an event occurring on April 22, 2019, it was a pivotal moment for Tesla, seeking to layout their existing AI efforts, the progress thereof, and where those vaunted AI efforts are headed).

Why do the restructuring?

Let's consider what might be the underlying basis for the restructuring effort, along with speculating about what can go right and what can potentially go wrong.

Overall, it's a boon or bust time for the Tesla Autopilot capabilities.

At the Tesla Investor Autonomy Day, Musk and the Tesla Autopilot team made some rather bold claims about what Autopilot can do today and what it will be doing in the future. Critics thought that the asserted timelines of being presumably at a fully autonomous car, considered a Level 5, within the end of this year or perhaps by the second quarter of next year to be nearly beyond belief. Generally, there was insufficient evidence presented to validate this incredible prediction.

To some, it would be like running a marathon, which the best in the world can do in about 2 hours, and suddenly suggesting that you'll be at the finish line in just thirty minutes, somehow skirting past all known laws of nature and physics. It's a jaw-dropping kind of declaration, especially if there isn't any substantive evidence showcased to support a potential world-record breaking projected achievement.

At this point, it's a wait-and-see status.

Meanwhile, if we try to read the tea leaves (conjecture), within the firm there might have been a realization that the dreamed for eclipsing of the laws of nature might need a second look. As such, perhaps triggering an impetus to resort to the restructuring tool and see what a restructuring exertion can achieve.

Some believe that a telltale sign was possibly signaled by the late start of the Tesla Investor Autonomy Day event (it got underway about 30 minutes late, with no particular explanation for the delay). A subtle aspect, admittedly, possibly benign, possibly more telling.

Let me share with you what sometimes happens leading up to the moments before big announcements by firms and how things can occasionally get gummed up.

In my having done consulting work with firms that develop AI software and were undertaking a major announcement summit, I've often witnessed first-hand that the CEO is brought up-to-speed just shortly before the public presentation and they can sometimes be taken aback, surprised at what is about to take place.

They might not have been in-the-loop to have already known what was real versus not real, they might have not been told about any bad news because who wants to be the bearer of bad news, they might have been in a bubble of believing something else and then when the rubber comes to meet the road it turns out there's a gap between their vision and what is real, etc.

This then becomes a gut-wrenching, chaotic fire drill of time-pressured back-and-forth among the team and the CEO to figure out what should and should not be said at the presentation, which can force the announcement to either be delayed or put aside for the moment.

But, the visibility of the announced event is often so overwhelming that the show must go on, and thus arm-twisting compromises are reached about what to say, imploring the team to keep-it-together for just a few hours, even if produces a muddled message or overstates the matter-at-hand.

How AI Software Teams Are Not Amenable To Restructuring

Unlike restructuring something relatively straightforward like a factory assembly plant operation, attempts to restructure a software development team, and especially one that is working on advanced AI systems, can be rather problematic. These are usually highly educated, highly skilled AI experts, considered in very high-demand as topnotch knowledge workers or white collars (versus blue-collar workers), if you will.

I recall one company wherein the CEO asked to meet with me privately and he had drawn-up on a sheet of paper a restructure that he had in mind for his budding AI team, a rough-sketch outline that had all kinds of wild circles and arrows, which it turns out upon discussion with him had little to do with actual AI skillsets and capabilities. Instead, it was based entirely on the CEO's perceptions of the respective *personalities* of the team members, since he knew little of anything about AI or what it takes to organize a team of AI specialists.

Not an especially suitable way to do a restructuring.

Here are a few downsides of what can happen when restructuring an AI team:

• Your top AI talent opts to walk across the street and go work someplace else since they are in high demand and aren't enamored of the new structure (often losing your star keepers).

• The new structure of the AI team creates confusion as to what was being done by whom, before the restructure, and who now has that responsibility, meaning that parts of the AI system might get short-shrift or fall between the resultant gaps.

• Pressure to have the restructured AI team catch-up with the dreamed-of vision can lead to cutting corners on the AI development or testing, spurring the inclusion of untoward software bugs or releasing software that isn't fully cooked.

• AI team members assigned to someone else's prior code aren't aware of key assumptions and under the intensity of making new progress are apt to assume that the code works, even though the original AI developer might have been expecting they would have had time to perfect the code (thus, it's incomplete or has other maladies, and the brain drain by losing the other AI talent leaves the rest in the dark).

• It becomes hard to hire anew topnotch AI talent to join the team since word spreads in the AI community that the team has become a chaotic spasm of desperate attempts to get the ship righted, though doing so without sufficient aplomb.

Conclusion

It is not yet publicly stated as to the full extent of how the Tesla Autopilot team restructuring has been undertaken.

Meanwhile, there has been a mixed "outsiders" reaction to the reported restructuring of the Tesla Autopilot team, including some that feel that things weren't moving at the pace that Musk desired and so it was about time to kick some butts into gear, while others are worried that the AI software is going to take a heavy hit and become less capable rather than more capable.

With these kinds of restructurings, it is difficult to ascertain whether the outcome will be a bright and better future or whether it will become one of doom-and-gloom, so it looks like we'll just have to wait and keep our eyes peeled

CHAPTER 13

RIGGED VIDEOS

AND

AI SELF-DRIVING CARS

CHAPTER 13

RIGGED VIDEOS

AND

AI SELF-DRIVING CARS

Magicians are said to be honor bound not to reveal how magic tricks are performed. The idea is to preserve the illusion that the magic is, well, quite magical. I'm not going to speculate about whether prestidigitators are using the dark-arts or simply clever sleight of hand, but I will tell you that when you watch those now ubiquitous video clips of driverless cars driving around neighborhoods and on our byways, there could very well be some behind-the-scenes skullduggery going on.

In some cases, those enthralling and astounding "sizzle reels" have been carefully staged to provide that oh-so-good feeling that autonomous cars are here-and-now, or that we're within inches of having them. It is actually pretty easy to portray driverless cars in that kind of light.

You, the viewer, aren't able to look around the corners to see what might be actually happening, similar to being forced to sit still in front of a stage when a magician makes that elephant disappear (spoiler alert: magicians usually don't want you to get out of your chair and come look anywhere around or underneath the stage).

I want to though clarify that I am not suggesting that all such videos and all such driverless car makers are purposely trying to pull the wool over your eyes. Many of the videos were made with great sincerity. Imagine that you've been slaving away at trying to craft and field a self-driving driverless car, and it is with great excitement and morale boosting to show-off what you've accomplished. I say, here, here.

I'm going to herein layout a handy list of selected "sweet sixteen" items for you to keep at top-of-mind when you watch a driverless car in-action video. Use the list to assess the overall indication of how truly autonomous that alleged driverless car really is.

Some Further Helpful Background

Before we jump into the list of elements, I do want to profusely emphasize that those genuine-aiming driverless car video-clip showcases should keep coming, thank you.

I say this because it is quite helpful for others in the industry to get a glimpse at what their fellow autonomous car makers are doing, which otherwise things are extensively cloaked in tremendous secrecy (as tightly as anything the CIA might be doing, it seems). The value of the technological wizardry is massive, and the desire to get there first in terms of arriving at driverless cars is equally enormous.

Of course, there is also the intense pressure by those investing billions into these innovations that spurs an impetus to present the latest progress and let the world know that the monies are being well-spent.

Indeed, some of those wizardry looking videos are perhaps done to shake-up the competition. Maybe you can get a competitor to toss in the towel, under the assumption they are way behind you, and give up on their self-driving car dreams.

Or, it can get others to decide that it might be better to get into bed with your efforts, forming a type of coopetition arrangement (competitors that cooperate), for which the autonomous car niche has already become web-like interconnected and infused.

So, for those that are popping out these videos like vines, don't get angry at me regarding my wanting to reveal some of the chicanery that takes place from time-to-time. Nor get angry at me that I'm aiming to inform the public about what they are seeing – I claim it is reasonable and fair to forewarn the public that seeing (these videos) is not necessarily equated to believing these videos.

In fact, I would assert that those automakers and tech firms that are legitimately proud of their genuine self-driving car work would welcome my pointing out how to best gauge what's real and what's not. Why should your bona fide efforts be compared equally to ones that have sought to put make-up on a pig, as they say. For true craftsmen and craftswomen, there's nothing more irksome than having the uninitiated layperson fail to distinguish between topnotch finely crafted work and something that's a shoddy piece of junk.

The Elements To Be Watchful About

Let's first agree that the driverless car video that you might be opting to look at hopefully (presumably) depicts a real car on a real road. If you are watching a self-driving car video that's apparently an animation or a clever CGI, I trust that you can weed those out right away as not depicting a real-world in-action autonomous car of some kind. A concept-oriented video is certainly interesting to watch, but it does not provide much down-to-earth confidence about what can actually be accomplished today.

Here's my list of elements to be cognizant of:

1. *Daylight versus nighttime.* Generally, it is much easier for a driverless car to strut during daylight, when there is plentiful light to ease the task of detecting the road and surrounding objects. If you watch an autonomous car zipping around in a video and it is a daylight version, you cannot assume that the self-driving car can maneuver as adroitly at nighttime.

2. *No traffic versus claustrophobic traffic.* Watch as the driverless car moves along and look for any nearby traffic. Often, the video was shot when there wasn't any other substantive number of human-driven cars nearby. Who knows what the autonomous car might do when amongst a crazed set of everyday drivers?

3. *Open roads versus complex convoluted roads.* Are the roads traveled upon by the self-driving car those country-living serene byways that are elegantly shaped or are they the real-world roads that you and I have to deal with involving maniacal crisscrossing nightmares, one-ways, and roads devised by some form of lunacy.

4. *No weather or adverse weather.* Not a cloud in the sky, it's a beautiful day for a driverless car romp. Yes, but what happens when the skies darken, rain floods down upon the earth, and otherwise the autonomous car needs to contend with something called "weather" (you know what I mean).

5. *No pedestrians versus pedestrians galore.* Sometimes the videos seem like they were filmed while all humans were told to stay inside their homes due to a zombie apocalypse. Real-world situations involve gobs of pedestrians, including jaywalkers, loose dogs, you name it.

6. *Smooth roads versus potholed roads.* I swear that some of the videos got the local city transportation department to urgently redo the streets and cover-up any potholes or other maladies, how nice of them. Let's see the driverless car deal with real-world bone-jarring stuff.

7. *Definitive markings versus faded/non-existent markings.* An autonomous car that primarily depends upon lane markings is vulnerable to normal roads that have faded or often non-existent ones.

8. *Pre-mapped versus partial/no mapping.* Some believe that driverless cars will only do well if they have a detailed pre-mapping available, while others believe that's a kind of unreliable crutch.

9. *Already driven versus first-time driven.* For some self-driving cars, the automaker or tech firm has to train the AI by driving on the particular road over-and-over, but this would seem to be an unsettling kind of requirement for truly autonomous cars.

10. *Geofenced versus open-borders.* Many of the autonomous car efforts are being purposely geofenced to an area that has been extensively pre-mapped and then driven over-and-over, which obviously is a restrictive kind of driving that humans don't need to do.

11. *No passenger instructions versus passenger requests.* When you are a passenger in a car that's driven by a human, you can say things like slow down, so that you can see the pretty bed of roses up ahead, or you might ask to pull into that drive-thru fast-food eatery for a quick burger while on-the-go. The AI of a truly autonomous car ought to be able to handle those passenger uttered requests.

12. *Snippet of the journey versus the full journey.* You watch a 15-second video-clip and the self-driving car drives like a champ, but maybe a few seconds later it has gotten itself into a bind and the back-up human driver had to perform a disengagement (taking over control). Be wary of carefully chosen snippets that show just the best and nothing of the rest.

13. *One-act play versus a multi-act play.* Mainly, you'll see an autonomous car that goes from point A to point B. Human drivers do more, they go from point A to point B, pick-up their kids from school, then go to point C, drop off one of them at the baseball field, then to point D, drop one off at the piano lessons, etc.

14. *Unencumbered path versus Encumbered path.* You are driving along and there's roadwork taking place, so you have to find a different way to get to work. Most of the driverless car videos seem to have all the luck and never encounter encumbered roadway issues. Can I live there?

15. *Ordinary encounters versus edge case encounters.* The other day, a family of ducks waddled onto the roadway as I was driving nearby to a local park. Some would say that this is an edge case, also referred to as a corner case, meaning it rarely happens. Autonomous cars cannot focus solely on the ordinary encounters, they need to be ready and able to deal with edge cases too.

16. *Easy-going driving versus crunch-oriented driving.* Usually, the driverless car doesn't seem to have a care in the world and takes its sweet time getting from point A to point B. That's not what most of us face. It's a dog-eat-dog world and driving is no exception.

Conclusion

There's your handy list of the "sweet sixteen" of criteria or characteristics to help be a myth buster when watching an alleged driverless car that's been captured on video. There are more aspects to look for, but I've aimed to boil the list down to a manageable number.

In quick recap:

• *Easiest set:* Daylight, no traffic, open road, no weather, no pedestrians, smooth roads, definitive markings, pre-mapped, already driven, geofenced, no passenger instructions, snippet, one-act, unencumbered, ordinary encounters, and easy-going.

• *More challenging set:* Nighttime, claustrophobic traffic, complex convoluted roads, adverse weather, pedestrians galore, potholed roads, faded/no markings, partial/no mapping, first-time driven, open borders, passenger instructions, full journey, multi-acts, encumbered, edge case encounters, and crunch-oriented driving situations.

Next time you watch an autonomous car video, you be the judge

CHAPTER 14

STALLED CARS

AND

AI SELF-DRIVING CARS

CHAPTER 14

STALLED CARS

AND

AI SELF-DRIVING CARS

Here's a driving situation that I'm guessing most of us have all experienced at one time or another. You are driving along on a highway or freeway, moving at a relatively fast clip (say 60 miles per hour, the prevailing speed and as matched with other nearby cars), surrounded by a mild amount of traffic, but nothing so onerous as to bog down the overall flow of vehicles.

A car to your left unexpectedly decides to dart into your lane, cutting down on the distance you had from the car directly ahead of you. It's one of those situations wherein the driver seems to want to swiftly go across multiple lanes of traffic, perhaps belatedly realizing that there is an off-ramp coming soon that they want to reach, and they had not been astute enough to gradually make their way over to the rightmost lane.

The driver then makes another lane change, doing so into the lane to your right, now clearing the path ahead of you. Keep in mind that all of this is happening in a matter of a handful of seconds, everyone moving at 60+ mph during the course of this series of eye-blinkingly brief events.

Upon the driver having shifted into the lane to your right, you can now see more readily what's ahead of you in your particular lane. Here's the rub. Turns out that there is a car in your lane, up ahead of you, which has either come to a crawl or might even be entirely halted, possibly stalled on the highway or freeway. Because the other car had somewhat momentarily blocked your view, you had not been able to see that this stalled car was a menace-in-waiting to you and your car.

You don't know whether the driver that had cut in front of you might have seen the stalled car and decided to make a quick escape, or whether they were merely completing their effort to get over into the rightmost lane for purposes of exiting at the next off-ramp. Either way, that driver has left you now holding the bag (a dangerous one, for sure!).

Essentially, you've been handed a hot potato. As recap, you were zooming along in your lane, and there is a car sitting in your lane, motionless, waiting to get smashed into by you, which you had not detected until the last moment, partially due to an interloper.

This is the moment that many drivers hope will never arise, yet it likely happens to many drivers, possibly with some substantial frequency, particularly if you are a daily driver that puts ample mileage on your car while commuting to work (I encounter these kinds of situations about once or so every two weeks, during my hour and a half long commute each day, each way, for work).

Typically, you maneuver out of the situation, often barely, by the skin of your teeth, though with about 6,300,000 car accidents occurring annually in the United States, some proportion of car crashes are undoubtedly due to this kind of inadvertent setup.

In a reported recent incident, a Tesla on Autopilot (according to the driver) rammed into a stalled vehicle on a highway, doing so while the Tesla was moving along at a speed of around 60 mph, and the crash occurred in a manner akin to what I've just described as a driving scenario.

According to the driver of the Tesla, another car cut in front of him, staying there fleetingly, then moved rapidly over to the next lane, and within moments it became apparent that a car was stalled up ahead, and he and his Tesla were going to ram right into it, full force. He and his Tesla did so, and luckily he lived to tell the tale.

It might be instructive to consider how this kind of a crash occurred and what it portends for Tesla drivers using Autopilot, along with ramifications for autonomous self-driving driverless cars in general.

Diagnosing What Happens In Stalled Car Crashes

Let's take out our Sherlock Holmes magnifying glass and try to ferret out salient characteristics of these kinds of automobile-based death-defying (though sometimes death resulting) incidents.

As I earlier suggested, sometimes you can maneuver out of the situation, while other times there is not any viable recourse and you get pinned into ramming into the stalled car.

Consider these two key elements:

• *Specific context in the moment.* The context of the specific driving predicament is a big factor in what will transpire since it determines what options might be viable and which ones are not.

• *Driver mindset and actions.* The thinking processes and actions of the driver are another crucial consideration for how the circumstance will play out.

If you try to hit your brakes, the question arises as to whether you can come to a stop in time, though even if you cannot come to a halt soon enough to prevent ramming of the stalled car, at least if you can ratchet down speed off your car you are going to reduce the likely amount of danger and resultant damage that can occur when you rear-end the other vehicle.

Beyond dealing with the speed of your car, you might perhaps swerve into another lane, either to your left or to your right, allowing you to either avoid entirely the stalled car, or maybe only sideswiping it, rather than plowing into it head-on.

Of course, the swerving action might be blocked by other cars that are to your left or right. Or, you might be able to do the swerve, yet other cars in the left or right lanes will then be disrupted by your movement into their lanes, possibly getting them directly involved in the pending crash. This often results in a domino-like cascade of cars hitting each other, doing so to avoid the sudden swerve that you made.

From the driver's perspective, it is important to consider how much time did they have to take a potential avoidance kind of action and were they cognitively attune to have been able to use that time as best possible.

In other words, a human driver can be caught off-guard, and even if there was sufficient time to do something, the person might either become mentally confounded or be shocked into a state of being frozen, not sure of what to do, and potentially wasting those precious few seconds when an action might have made a significant difference to the outcome.

Now, let's add into this scenario the use of automation, focusing on Advanced Driver-Assistance Systems (ADAS), and see how that changes the picture.

Semi-Autonomous Cars And The Co-Shared Driving Task

When reviewing an incident involving ADAS, and especially for those cars that are considered semi-autonomous, meaning they are not yet at a true autonomous level, not being at Level 5, and in the case of the Tesla Autopilot being at a considered Level 2, you need to imagine that there are essentially two drivers of the car, the human driver and the semi-autonomous automation.

What did your co-shared semi-autonomous driving "partner" do?

In theory, the Tesla Autopilot should not have been susceptible to a mind-freeze that a human being might have and would have unemotionally and computationally calmly calculated the matter. This would involve detecting the object ahead, and interpreting that the object was not moving, and ascertaining that the Tesla was moving toward the stalled object and would intersect (badly) with it, and then try to figure out what action to take.

According to the reported incident, the Autopilot did not engage the brakes. If so, we should be asking, why not? As a minimum, at least the Automatic Emergency Braking (AEB) should presumably have engaged.

Also, apparently the Autopilot did not try to swerve the car and avoid or reduce the head-on impact, which once again we are left to ask why it did not do so? Was it because it failed to consider utilizing any quick-maneuver options? As a side note, the Tesla manual warns that the Autopilot might not well handle these kinds of situations, though I have more to say about that aspect in a moment herein.

This incident further raises the question as to whether or not Tesla ought to be using LIDAR, a mash-up of light and radar that is a sensory device used by nearly all other autonomous car makers. Would a LIDAR device have potentially aided in detecting the stalled car? It is possible that a LIDAR unit, especially if positioned on the top of the vehicle, would have had an added chance of detecting the upcoming calamity, providing what I refer to as an essential omnipresence capability for the automation attempting to aid in driving the car.

On another notable facet of the incident, the human driver says that there was insufficient time for him to react.

Let's make clear that this does not give the Autopilot a freebie in terms of suggesting that it too did not have time to react. The human driver might genuinely believe that he had insufficient time (he might be right, he might be mistaken), but the automation, working at the speed of onboard computers, could potentially have had time to do something.

Plus, we're removing the human mental coagulation time out of the equation when considering what the Autopilot automation system might have had time to do.

There is also a chance that the human driver might have assumed that the Autopilot was going to aid in the driving, doing so at this key or decisive moment, and thus the human driver might have instinctively delayed their own actions, spurred consciously or subconsciously under the assumption that their co-shared automation-based "driver" would come to their rescue.

Conclusion

Tesla typically points out in these kinds of incidents that it is the human driver that is responsible for the car, no matter what the Autopilot automation does or doesn't do.

That's a seemingly easy means to swipe away any possible limitations of the automation.

Plus, for human drivers, it is difficult to continually keep a mindset that you are presumably the captain of the ship, retaining ultimate responsibility, which is somewhat mentally undermined when you know that you have your second-in-command running things for you, the Autopilot, and then all of sudden, bam, turns out that you were supposed to be the one handling the controls (a Catch-22, as it were).

Furthermore, this kind of setup of Human-Machine Interaction (HMI) belies the aspect that the human driver might believe that the automation is going to do something, in spite of the human driver being informed possibly long-ago or as found in some owner's manual that they cannot rely upon the automation.

Human nature cannot be so readily overturned by merely telling someone to ignore their instincts or overcome what might have become an ingrained habit.

I have repeatedly forewarned that as we encounter the emergence of Level 2 with ADAS and Level 3 semi-autonomous cars coming into the marketplace, there will be a lot more of these kinds of incidents involving a co-shared human-machine driving effort that inevitably falters or fails to take what might have been suitable action to avoid or reduce a car crash.

Regrettably, get ready for more of this and brace yourself accordingly.

CHAPTER 15

PRINCETON SUMMIT

AND

AI SELF-DRIVING CARS

CHAPTER 15

PRINCETON SUMMIT

AND

AI SELF-DRIVING CARS

Professor Alain Kornhauser is a veritable force of nature when it comes to pursuing the cause of the mobility marginalized in the race toward producing and fielding autonomous cars.

Speaking with him at his annual Smart Driving Cars Summit that took place last week at Princeton University, it's the third one to-date (the next one is May 13-14, 2020), his determination and passion were quite evident, and while moderating this important event he managed to cajole and spur the esteemed speakers, keeping them on-track and intently focused on the crucial topics at-hand.

The tag line for the annual event is seeking safe, inclusive, affordable, energy efficient, and environmentally responsible on-demand 24/7 mobility for all people, especially the mobility marginalized.

That ambitious proclamation is what used to be called a BHAG, Big Hairy Audacious Goal, which in this case is unquestionably essential and laudable.

By his having assembled and in some cases roped-in top leaders in the relevant policy and regulatory areas, I was encouraged to see that there is a rising tide of interest in a matter that regrettably is not yet getting its due overall. Hearteningly, many of his former students that graduated under his tutelage have subsequently opted to further carry the banner on these efforts and were there to showcase various new research or inventions that they are bringing to the market, often entrepreneurially doing so.

For most of the myriad of autonomous cars conferences taking place these days, the usual focus is primarily on the rudiments of how to make driverless cars technologically ready to cruise our roadways. Meanwhile, the aspects of access and use of the emerging driverless mobility extraordinaire for everyone has not gotten nearly as much attention as it should.

Policy And Tech Are Inextricably Intertwined

In my view, if we don't design-in the appropriate technological facets for this use case, it will mean that those already mobility marginalized are bound to be placed even further behind, not being able to adequately benefit from self-driving cars.

And, looking further down-the-road to what will happen once initial driverless car adoption plays out, any after-the-fact efforts to retrofit autonomous cars for more encompassing access will undoubtedly be so burdensome that it will delay or hamper efforts to get things righted.

You might find of interest that there is an insider adage in the AI and systems field that it is less costly and more effective to design-in what you'll need in a system, at the front end of development, anticipating what you'll need or want later on, rather than waking up afterward and facing a gigantic bill and an overly arduous redo to make up for earlier oversights or omissions.

As described in one of my several books on AI, prudent and thoughtful upstream designs can handily accommodate downstream expansions and emergent realizations, while myopic pigeon-holed upstream designs tend to undermine and diminish downstream augmentations and newly discovered innovations.

Design for everyone at the get-go, it's a handy mantra for automakers and tech firms toiling away on devising autonomous cars.

Customer Journey Methodology Applies Here

Let's dig more deeply into how to bring to the forefront what must be done to devise greater access to autonomous cars for everyone.

First, as a helpful context for you, I tend to use a customer journey approach when developing AI systems for autonomous cars. This methodology consists of examining the key stages of undertaking travel or a journey when utilizing a driverless car, consisting of these seven core stages:

1. Hailing a driverless car
2. Approaching a nearing driverless car
3. Getting into a driverless car
4. Interacting with the AI during within the driverless car
5. Exigencies during the journey
6. Exiting from the driverless car
7. Departing away from the driverless car

At each stage, the human passenger has to be ready for the autonomous car and be able to work collaboratively with the AI system to ensure a safe and successful journey.

Likewise, and key to being mindful of forward-thinking design, the AI needs to be capable of undertaking this collaborative dance. The human passenger needs an AI system partner that knows what maneuvers to make and that can proactively aid in ensuring a safe end-to-end traveling journey for the human passenger.

One of the summit speakers, Dr. Cecilia Feeley, Transportation Autism Project Manager for the Center for Advanced Infrastructure and Transportation at Rutgers University, described research concentrating on those with autism and how an autonomous car would potentially interact with someone having ASD (Autism Spectrum Disorders). Consider the stages of my outlined customer journey and you can envision aspects of how the AI and the driverless car could be developed to accommodate such provisions. Automakers and AI developers need to put themselves into such shoes and provide designs that fit accordingly.

Speaking of innovative research on these topics, another speaker was Diana Furchtgott-Roth, Deputy Assistant Secretary for Research and Technology at the U.S. Department of Transportation (DOT). With about a billion dollars per year allocated by Congress to the DOT for research efforts relevant to the transportation milieu, she indicated that there is keen interest in having proposals covering the emerging frontier of making self-driving cars that can support the mobility marginalized. I urge driverless car researchers to pursue this funding opportunity and contribute to this budding application area.

Explainable AI Is Arising

Another vital research area involves an embryonic field of study known as explainable AI (usually referred to as XAI).

Many AI systems are based on Machine Learning or Deep Learning, typically consisting of large-scale or "deep" Artificial Neural Networks (ANN), mincing how neurons work and often becoming so computationally massive and web-like that they are seemingly inscrutable. This means that whatever answer or decision the AI renders, it is difficult to discern any logical basis for how the system arrived at its conclusions or actions.

Some decry that this leaves us at the mercy of essentially a black-box. It could be that the AI system has hidden biases, yet those biases are not sufficiently surfaced or dealt with. Worse still, for a real-time life-or-death AI system running a driverless car, there could be deeply embedded brittleness points that when encountered at the worst of times will cause the driving actions to go awry.

At the Summit, speaker Laura Kornhauser, co-founder of Stratyfy, described how explainable AI can be used to try and open the black-box, doing so to derive a logic-based means to understand what the AI is doing. By enabling an explainable AI capability, the otherwise mathematically opaque paths can be examined by human stakeholders.

Indeed, in the case of autonomous cars, I've previously indicated in my research that explainable AI will be crucial for shaping the intrinsic life-or-death decision making of self-driving systems. In another AI book of mine, I offer insights about how human trust will be a crucial element of autonomous car acceptance and adoption, including ways in which XAI can boost trustworthiness.

There is a philosophical yet indubitably practical ethical dilemma often described as the Trolley Problem, essentially indicating that we are all going to be relying on AI systems performing driving tasks that will need to make immediate choices between two adverse consequences, such as running over someone that has darted into the street versus swerving the passenger-occupied vehicle but then ramming into say a post or a large tree. Neither outcome desirable, but nonetheless a choice must be made.

Can we really just let a black-box that seemingly contains arcane, unsurfaced, and unknown-to-us embedded assumptions be rendering these choices?

I think not, and I've emphasized repeatedly that once these black-box unexplained AI systems become deployed, it will undoubtedly lead to public angst, plus a legal bonanza that will see the AI makers dragged into court, likely finding themselves on the losing end of having put into production systems that they cannot sufficiently explain how they work.

Conclusion

For those of you interested in hearing a podcast covering the Smart Driving Cars Summit highlights, I spoke with Fred Fishkin while at the event, the notable tech reporter and podcaster via his renowned Techstination, and he indicated that there's a podcast series he has been doing with Professor Kornhauser, so make sure to take a listen if you are further interested in these smart driving cars topics.

Overall, I encourage everybody to get onto the mobility-for-everyone bandwagon. All of us need to be on a mission of shaping autonomous cars that encompasses all, including the oft-neglected or forgotten mobility marginalized. It's a noble quest we can all join.

CHAPTER 16

BRITTLENESS

AND

AI SELF-DRIVING CARS

CHAPTER 16

BRITTLENESS

AND

AI SELF-DRIVING CARS

In my column of last Sunday, I analyzed a Tesla Autopilot incident involving a Tesla Model 3 that slammed into a stalled car on a highway, and readers subsequently asked me to do a follow-up to discuss the recently released study by *Consumer Reports* regarding the latest version of the Tesla Autopilot lane changing feature, which thusly I provide such an analysis herein.

In addition to that readership request, I also had some Tesla fans or supporters that expressed qualms that the piece last Sunday tended to focus on what might have gone awry in the incident, offering what they considered criticism of Tesla cars, and did not cover the positives about Tesla cars or Elon Musk's efforts.

In that regard, allow me a moment to emphasize that I believe that Tesla cars are overall a marvel of engineering and should receive accolades for having many bold and forward-thinking advances.

Likewise, Musk deserves tremendous credit for his entrepreneurial zeal and vision of what automobiles can become. In my business books on business leadership and especially entrepreneurship, and having consulted with many successful entrepreneurs, I typically point out that it takes a determined spirit and visionary to start with merely a dream and then build-up a company and a product that can achieve success in the marketplace.

That being said, I would also suggest that any entrepreneur aiming for long-term success and aspirations to transform an industry would most likely want to receive feedback about their product, allowing them to make changes and enhancements for ensuring long-term impact, including feedback that seems to be criticism (platitudes alone aren't likely to offer much value toward improving product deficiencies, which all products are bound to have).

It is my impression that Elon Musk is seeking to avoid having Tesla merely be a passing fad and instead he is presumably striving to offer a product that can make a sustained difference in the world. As cited in my research, successful entrepreneurs know that having a thin skin is not an option they can afford and instead must anticipate, and more so often reach out for at times unsettling feedback, propelling them toward achieving an even better product and a brighter long-lasting future for their efforts.

Just wanted to mention those aspects, and now let's get into the matter-at-hand.

Lane Changes As A Fundamental Driving Maneuver

One of the most frequently performed driving tasks by human drivers involves making lane changes.

You do so all the time, often without having to overtly think about how you are doing so.

Typically, you glance over your shoulder to see if the lane that you want to change into has an opening, you turn-on your blinker to signal that you are intending to make a lane change, you then steer the car into the other lane, and you usually then match the speed and pace of the cars that you've now entered into the stream of.

You might do these lane changing acts dozens of time while driving to work each day or while heading to your local mall to go shopping. It is a routine action when driving a car.

Admittedly, sometimes you might get sloppy about such efforts, or you might see other drivers that aren't quite as civil and proper when making lane changes. There's the driver that doesn't turn-on their turn indicator and just seemingly leaps into another lane, doing so without any forewarning. There's the driver that cuts off the traffic in the targeted lane and doesn't match the speed or pace when making the lane change, causing a sea of braking lights and consternation from other drivers. And so on.

If you've ever been with a teenage novice driver, it can be an eye-opening experience that awakens you to how difficult making lane changes can really be.

Though you've gotten used to making lane changes, a novice driver is unsure about the matter and might even be a bit terrified trying to do so. They realize that at any moment they could inadvertently crash into another car as they attempt to perform the lane change. Or, another car could crash into them because of poorly executing the lane change.

How do you feel when you are in a car as a passenger and have a driver that appears to be unsure about making lane changes? I'd bet that you are on-edge, sweating out each time that a lane change is undertaken. Your heart races and your nerves get frayed. It makes a driving journey into a horrifying experience.

According to a recent study by Consumer Reports, the Tesla Autopilot feature that was recently updated and can now (allegedly) do an automatic lane change without needing human driver assistance is akin to that kind of unsure lane changer.

Furthermore, Consumer Reports indicates that "the automatic lane-change function raises serious safety concerns" and hasn't been "vetted properly" before putting it into use on our public roadways.

What Happens By The Automation When Making A Lane Change

Let's closely examine why the lane changing feature is reported as untoward.

Any semi-autonomous car, such as the Tesla on Autopilot, which is considered a Level 2 and not a fully autonomous self-driving car (that's a Level 5), uses various sensory devices to try and detect the traffic that is nearby to the car.

There are likely multiple cameras that are streaming in visual images of the other vehicles and roadway artifacts such as street signs, curbs, lane markers, etc.

Within the AI system, there is an attempt to perform vision processing that seeks to make sense of the images, identifying each pertinent artifact as seen in the visually captured data, and discern which artifacts are important for the driving act and which are not particularly important at the time. A tree that's standing some twenty feet away from the roadway is probably not as crucial to discern as might be a car that's in the lane next to you and coming up upon you at a fast rate of speed.

In addition to cameras, there are often also radar sensors involved. These radar units send out radar waves that bounce off objects and return a signal to the radar unit, sometimes, allowing for the AI to gauge the distance to objects, sometimes, depending upon the capabilities of the radar sensor and the kind of objects nearby to the car.

Keep in mind that the cameras and radar are presumably operating in real-time and there isn't much time available for the AI system to process the data being captured about the street scene surrounding the car.

The AI undertakes sensor fusion, wanting to combine together the myriad of sensors and their data, and uses the results to analyze the roadway situation, along with determining whether a driving maneuver is possible or not. When you make a lane change, you glance over your shoulder, doing so for just a second or two, and then opt to move into the lane, assuming that your glance led you to believe that there is an appropriate opening in the other lane for you to steer into. In theory, the AI system is trying to do the same thing, using its cameras and other sensory devices.

When Consumer Reports tested the Tesla Model 3 on Autopilot using the newer Navigate feature for making automatic lane changes, the test drivers in the Tesla's reported that the automatic lane changes were often done in an unsafe manner, such as cutting off cars in the other lane. At times, the testers took over control of the automatic lane changing due to fears that the Tesla was about to get into a car accident.

The rearward-facing cameras apparently seemed to be unable to sufficiently detect fast approaching cars in those other lanes, thus, the AI would seemingly falsely believe that the lane change was viable and safe, in spite of the potential for causing a collision or at least being disruptive of other car traffic nearby.

Here are some key reasons why this can happen:

• It could be that the camera is "seeing" the other fast approaching cars but not appropriately processing the images and therefore does not put two-plus-two together to discern that by making the lane change the Tesla will be disrupting the forecasted path of the other cars (it's an AI action planning flaw or omission).

• Or, it could be that the camera is not able to adequately gauge the speed of the car in the other lane, perhaps only noting that the car is back far enough to allow for an opening to make the lane change, but not realizing that the car is fast approaching and will be in the same spot as the lane change once the Tesla maneuvers into the lane (a sensory-related limitation).

As I've discussed previously, Elon Musk and Tesla have chosen to not make use of LIDAR, unlike nearly all other autonomous car developers, and per my earlier indication that at some point it might become apparent that the lack of LIDAR is a substantive detriment, it is quite possible that this seeming inability to sufficiently detect a fast approaching car in another lane is potentially such an example.

Lane Changes Often Tied To Passing Another Car

One of the reasons that you might make a lane change is to get around a car that's in front of you.

Suppose there is a car ahead of you that is lolling along and going slower than the speed limit, and you want to use another lane to proceed around that plodder. Customarily, you would make a lane change into the lane to your left, proceed ahead of the other car, and then get back into the lane, now ahead of that slower moving car, doing so hopefully safely and without being a dolt as you did so.

You might at times be tempted to make the same overtaking or passing maneuver by going around the plodding car via the lane to the right, often considered the inside lane, but this is a driving maneuver that is roundly considered ill-advised.

By convention, drivers know about passing to the left and tend to expect it, while passing to the right is not as expected, plus in some states it is actually illegal to pass to the right. Therefore, whenever you might attempt to pass another car by swinging into a lane to the right, you are raising the risks of something going awry, along with potentially committing an illegal driving act.

Per the Consumer Reports testing, the testers indicated that the Autopilot automatic lane changer would often undertake a passing or overtaking action to the right, seemingly without a care in the world as to the ill-advised nature of it, and nor apparently realizing that it would be an illegal act in some states.

Machine Learning As Both Useful And Problematic

Elon Musk and Tesla have repeatedly emphasized that they use their collected driving data from the Tesla cars to aid in shaping the AI driving capabilities of their cars. This is touted as a key competitive advantage by them, due to having thousands upon thousands of Tesla's on the roadways and being able to access the data that those cars have collected.

When using Machine Learning, an AI system attempts to find patterns in large sets of data and then leverages those patterns for subsequent actions that it will undertake. Thus, having large data sets is handy and indeed vital for using Machine Learning techniques and technologies.

Here's the rub.

If you have tons of data that has human drivers that make well-advised lane changes, but it also contains data of human drivers that make ill-advised lane changes, the AI can inadvertently be led into assuming that both the well-advised driving practice is sound and that the ill-advised driving practice is also sound.

Today's AI has no kind of common-sense reasoning to know any better and assumes that whatever patterns are found are acceptable.

In short:

• It could be that the willingness to make lane changes that cut-off other fast approaching cars might be a "learned" behavior by the AI from the set of data being used to identify driving maneuvers.

• It could be that the apparent use of passing or overtaking cars to their right is also a "learned" behavior that the AI derived from the set of data being used.

Without access to Tesla's collected data set, there is no ready way to know whether the weaknesses and unsafe efforts of the automatic lane changer are due to the sensory device limitations, which it could be, or whether it might be due to the AI system that has used brittle Machine Learning and picked-up bad habits. Or, it could be both aspects as a double whammy.

Conclusion

Imagine that you sat with a novice teenage driver and told them to merely mimic whatever else they experienced while driving a car, such as drivers that roll through stop signs, or run through red lights, or make dicey lane changes, and how scary a driver that teenager might be.

For autonomous car developers that eschew any kind of programmatic approach to developing AI for driving, they need to understand that relying solely on Machine Learning can be problematic, given that the AI won't be able to gauge what is sensible or reasonable, which at least even a novice teenager could ultimately figure out.

Though Tesla asserts that it is the responsibility of the human driver to ensure that an automatic lane change is properly executed by the AI, I've deprecated many times that a human driver of a semi-autonomous car is likely to allow themselves to become mentally adrift of the AI actions and fall into a mental reliance trap that won't either catch the AI flaws in-time or that will be stuck in the middle of an unsafe maneuver that cannot be recovered from.

Co-sharing the driving task with a human driver and automation of this sort is bound to produce untoward results for the human driver, along with the occupants of whatever cars they might crash into, and we are allowing ourselves to be part of a public roadway experiment encompassing daily hidden dangers.

CHAPTER 17

MERGERS

AND

AI SELF-DRIVING CARS

CHAPTER 17

MERGERS

AND

AI SELF-DRIVING CARS

Yesterday was the Monday of Memorial Day weekend in the United States, traditionally a day of attention to matters of the heart and an otherwise quiet news day. For the automotive industry, it turns out that yesterday was a rather newsy revelation day, involving the announcement by Fiat Chrysler Automobiles (FCA) of their interest in merging with Renault.

In a sense, the proposed approach suggests a merger of equals in that the pitch offers a 50-50 merger, including an equal split of the shares among the shareholders of the two firms.

Two behemoths, possibly combining together, maybe even peaceably so. Now that's news. Also, given the seemingly daily talk of automotive firms entering into various alliances and cooperative agreements in often pinpointed or narrow ways, let's be clear that this is much more so than a casual dating relationship being proposed, it's a betrothed full-on marriage.

FCA says that there won't be any plant closures due to the merger, which right away can cause some head-scratching about where the benefits will arise as a result of the combination. According to FCA, they claim that the key benefits are improvements in capital efficiencies and hastened speed of development.

There's a particular passage in their proposal that I find of keen interest: "The case for combination is also strengthened by the need to take bold decisions to capture at scale the opportunities created by the transformation of the auto industry in areas like connectivity, electrification and autonomous driving."

Essentially, it boils down to autonomous cars made me do it.

And in many ways, I agree.

The advent of autonomous self-driving driverless cars is going to shake-up the automotive industry and those automakers that aren't looking ahead to that day are going to find themselves and their firms on the losing end of the upcoming disruption and transformation. Though I'm not one of those that says the sky is falling, I do think that the tea leaves make it pretty apparent that the conventional automobile is gradually going to become unwanted and instead the autonomous car is going to become king.

Let's unpack the aspects of how FCA is currently pursuing driverless cars, and likewise how Renault is pursuing driverless cars, and see if we can figure out what their combined approach to driverless cars might become.

How The Merger Might Involve A Fusion Of Their Driverless Car Efforts

Having been a management consultant to many Mergers & Acquisitions (M&A) efforts, along with having at times been a corporate officer and executive in a company initiating an M&A or serving in firms that were on the receiving end of an M&A deal, I'll go ahead and offer some speculation about what might take place with the FCA and Renault merger, especially focusing on the self-driving cars side of things.

Allow me a moment to lay out my five essential strategies that could occur with their driverless car efforts, ranging from a minimal amount of merger to a more substantive composition of merging:

• Self-Driving Cars Remain Distinct.

One approach involves allowing each of their respective autonomous car efforts to keep going as they have been, unchanged and unfettered by the overarching merger of the companies. This might also mean that a hunger-games competition might arise internally, wherein FCA's driverless car efforts try to showcase they are better than Renault's, or that Renault's autonomous car teams attempt to demonstrate that they are the better of the two. It could become a winner take all, down the road, after the merger dust settles.

• Loose Collaboration on Driverless Cars.

Another approach involves purposely getting their respective driverless car efforts to be open to sharing with each other. This is the classic two-heads being better than one. This can sometimes succeed, but it can also create tension as to which way is considered the more optimal path, which tends to get escalated to the top ranks of the firm if not worked out at the lower levels.

• Interweave Their Self-Driving Cars Efforts.

In this approach, the two try to combine together their respective autonomous car efforts, which seems to be the idea pitched in the merger proposal, presumably leading to a larger scale and untold synergies that each separately would not otherwise achieve. Ironically, when one firm takes over another, the decisions about what lives and what gets junked is usually pretty easy (the buying firm makes those choices).

For this instance of presumed co-equals, there will be tough decisions ahead about the autonomous car technologies and systems that will prevail and which will be set to the side, and I'd anticipate some gut-wrenching internal angst and difficulties as those decisions are being made.

• Anoint One Driverless Car Effort As The Chosen One.

During the merger due diligence process, it could be that a decision is made to keep moving forward on one of the driverless car efforts and to close down the other.

This doesn't necessarily mean that the AI developers and engineers in the less-preferred effort will be out on the streets, since these days firms are scrambling to get such talent, and by-and-large it could be that they would be transitioned into the chosen effort. The downside can be that some could harbor their old ways and not be willing to adopt the driverless car efforts they are now wedded into (AI specialists often are dogmatic about their viewpoints and dogged when it comes to changing their ways).

• **Embark Upon An Entirely New Approach.**

There's the off chance that a decision could be made to scuttle the existing FCA driverless car efforts and likewise dash the Renault driverless car efforts, aiming toward some entirely different approach. I could speculate about what the other approach might be, but I really doubt that such a radical act will take place and it seems much more prudent that they would continue with either or both of their existing paths.

Now that we've got a map or framework of the various ways to merge together their autonomous car efforts, let's review what their present status is.

Where FCA And Renault Each Stand On Autonomous Cars To-Date

I'd say it is widely known within the realm of autonomous cars that FCA's former CEO Sergio Marchionne, who sadly passed away last year, had been pursuing a driverless car strategy that was at times criticized by the pundits that argued for an all-in stratagem.

Marchionne's viewpoint was to try and spread his risks associated with making investments into autonomous cars. It got him labeled by some as a "cheapskate" or a "penny pincher" when it came to pursuing driverless cars, but I had argued that those proffering such biting accusations were actually somewhat close-minded about the kinds of arduous choices top leaders often have to make in this space.

You have to realize that developing a true Level 5 self-driving driverless autonomous car is akin to a moonshot.

Per Apple's CEO, Tim Cook, autonomous cars have been likened to the mother of all systems projects. He's right.

Indeed, in spite of some others that keep trying to suggest that Level 5 is easy and imminent, I'd readily bet they are wrong. As such, Marchionne knew that it would be a gamble to sink all his chips into only one venture or one approach, and he opted to try and balance out his odds. For those that don't play poker, putting all your stakes into one pot can be a potential giant money maker or can be a total bust. Some prefer to be moderate in how they play the game.

I believe he well-articulated that he wanted to be in-the-game and as a result undertook a three-pronged stance, involving Waymo, BMW, and Aptiv.

FCA has partnered with Waymo, the furthest along on aiming at a Level 5, and the partnership has led to the Chrysler Pacifica minivan becoming a favored star for establishing and testing driverless car technologies. As a plug-in hybrid, it provides the kind of EV and battery capabilities needed for autonomous car tech, acting as an especially suitable platform, and the size and space within the vehicle accommodates the onboard systems and sensors, along with allowing for passengers and a human back-up driver or engineer.

As widely touted last year, Waymo indicated they are going to obtain 62,000 more of the Chrysler Pacifica minivans on their quest these next several years to expand their public roadway tryouts. Marchionne wisely aligned with Waymo CEO John Krafcik, seemingly being of one spirit that the road to self-driving cars needs to be safe, efficient, and realistic. Waymo's "conservative" efforts to achieve driverless cars, relative to others that are taking a more dramatic and wild-leap approach, fit well with FCA's direction via Marchionne.

Let's consider the BMW partnership and the Aptiv partnership, each entity being in the pursuit of the multiple levels of semi-autonomous and autonomous cars.

With BMW, reportedly the FCA aim has tended to involve Level 3 technologies, often referred to as Advanced Driver-Assistance Systems (ADAS), particularly for premium kinds of cars. And with Aptiv, formerly Delphi Automotive, the focus reportedly seems to be toward Level 2+ kinds of ADAS and doing so for a broader range of cars, beyond the premium scope of the BMW partnership.

Though the BMW and Aptiv arrangements appear on the surface as somewhat narrow, you need to consider that Marchionne was likely hedging his bets, meaning that by having an arrangement with Waymo, and with BMW, and with Aptiv, he could potentially swing further into any particular one if he thought the timing and results would be warranted in doing so, such as if one of them seemed to falter, or if any of the particular relationships somehow soured.

You might be wondering how does the strategy of Renault compare to FCA's?

Renault has offered some rather extravagant concept cars for the future of driverless vehicles, including their EZ-Ultimo and their EZ-Go.

The EZ-Ultimo is a driverless luxury limousine, offering a so-called first-class lounge as the interior, encompassing ornate wood paneling, genuine marble, and blocked-out windows to offer privacy for those seated within (it only seats 3 people). The EZ-Go seats 6 people and as a concept car is envisioned at a Level 4, presumably being a robo-taxi ridesharing vehicle, providing a glass door that rises and a ramp for accommodating the disabled. These are concept cars and some pundits like the designs and others eschew the designs.

Meanwhile, at the Viva Tech 2019 conference in this month of May, the Renault Zoe Cab was touted, along with an indication that it will be utilized for tryouts as part of the Paris-Saclay Autonomous Lab Project. The targeted Level 4 car can seat 3 passengers and one safety or back-up driver.

Besides their own self-driving car efforts, Renault is also part of an alliance with Nissan, which has its own self-driving car efforts. Industry figures indicate that Renault owns 43.4% of Nissan, while Nissan owns 15% of Renault.

The alliance is somewhat further complicated since Mitsubishi is also another partner with the Renault-Nissan arrangement, making it the Renault-Nissan-Mitsubishi alliance, and of course, the recent difficulties facing the former Renault-Nissan Alliance CEO Carlos Ghosn have undoubtedly added to the internal activities.

In any case, earlier this year it was widely reported that Waymo and the Renault-Nissan-Mitsubishi alliance were aiming to forge an arrangement for jointly undertaking autonomous car development.

Conclusion

Under my strategic category of self-driving cars "remain distinct" stratagem, FCA's CEO Mike Manley could potentially continue Marchionne's hedging-bets strategy, meaning that he would continue the Waymo relationship, plus continue with the BMW and Aptiv angles, while also having the Renault-Nissan-Mitsubishi approaches underway too. That might seem like too many cooks in the kitchen.

Or, he might go toward the "loose collaboration" stratagem, perhaps forging ahead with the earlier proposed Waymo and Renault-Nissan-Mitsubishi arrangement, though this would seem like a lessening potentially of the hedging-bets notion if it portends that the BMW relationship might be lessened or the Aptiv relationship might be lessened. Some might suggest that this could be part of a new boldness under his administration.

It seems unlikely that all the autonomous car eggs of the FCA and Renault merger would be placed into only one basket, which is the "anoint a chosen one" stratagem, and nor does it seem that an entirely new or different approach would be crafted and somehow completely gut or discard what has already been undertaken.

One thing we can seemingly be assured is that Mike Manley is willing to take bold steps, as evidenced via the valorous proposed merger with Renault, and it would seem that his business ideology is one that is going to be embracing boldness.

As such, in reading the tea leaves, we can anticipate that whichever direction he goes on autonomous cars, and in presumed joint dialogue with Renault CEO Thierry Bollore, he fully gets the notion that a tsunami-like transformation is inextricably coming to the automotive industry and he's going to undertake whatever tough decisions need to be made about avidly pursuing the vaunted autonomous self-driving driverless car.

APPENDIX

APPENDIX A
TEACHING WITH THIS MATERIAL

The material in this book can be readily used either as a supplemental to other content for a class, or it can also be used as a core set of textbook material for a specialized class. Classes where this material is most likely used include any classes at the college or university level that want to augment the class by offering thought provoking and educational essays about AI and self-driving cars.

In particular, here are some aspects for class use:

o   Computer Science. Studying AI, autonomous vehicles, etc.

o   Business. Exploring technology and it adoption for business.

o   Sociology. Sociological views on the adoption and advancement of technology.

Specialized classes at the undergraduate and graduate level can also make use of this material.

For each chapter, consider whether you think the chapter provides material relevant to your course topic. There is plenty of opportunity to get the students thinking about the topic and force them to decide whether they agree or disagree with the points offered and positions taken. I would also encourage you to have the students do additional research beyond the chapter material presented (I provide next some suggested assignments they can do).

RESEARCH ASSIGNMENTS ON THESE TOPICS

Your students can find background material on these topics, doing so in various business and technical publications. I list below the top ranked AI related journals. For business publications, I would suggest the usual culprits such as the Harvard Business Review, Forbes, Fortune, WSJ, and the like.

Here are some suggestions of homework or projects that you could assign to students:

a) <u>Assignment for foundational AI research topic</u>: Research and prepare a paper and a presentation on a specific aspect of Deep AI, Machine Learning, ANN, etc. The paper should cite at least 3 reputable sources. Compare and contrast to what has been stated in this book.

b) <u>Assignment for the Self-Driving Car topic</u>: Research and prepare a paper and Self-Driving Cars. Cite at least 3 reputable sources and analyze the characterizations. Compare and contrast to what has been stated in this book.

c) <u>Assignment for a Business topic</u>: Research and prepare a paper and a presentation on businesses and advanced technology. What is hot, and what is not? Cite at least 3 reputable sources. Compare and contrast to the depictions in this book.

d) <u>Assignment to do a Startup:</u> Have the students prepare a paper about how they might startup a business in this realm. They must submit a sound Business Plan for the startup. They could also be asked to present their Business Plan and so should also have a presentation deck to coincide with it.

You can certainly adjust the aforementioned assignments to fit to your particular needs and the class structure. You'll notice that I ask for 3 reputable cited sources for the paper writing based assignments. I usually steer students toward "reputable" publications, since otherwise they will cite some oddball source that has no credentials other than that they happened to write something and post it onto the Internet. You can define "reputable" in whatever way you prefer, for example some faculty think Wikipedia is not reputable while others believe it is reputable and allow students to cite it.

The reason that I usually ask for at least 3 citations is that if the student only does one or two citations they usually settle on whatever they happened to find the fastest. By requiring three citations, it usually seems to force them to look around, explore, and end-up probably finding five or more, and then whittling it down to 3 that they will actually use.

I have not specified the length of their papers, and leave that to you to tell the students what you prefer. For each of those assignments, you could end-up with a short one to two pager, or you could do a dissertation length paper. Base the length on whatever best fits for your class, and the credit amount of the assignment within the context of the other grading metrics you'll be using for the class.

I mention in the assignments that they are to do a paper and prepare a presentation. I usually try to get students to present their work. This is a good practice for what they will do in the business world. Most of the time, they will be required to prepare an analysis and present it. If you don't have the class time or inclination to have the students present, then you can of course cut out the aspect of them putting together a presentation.

If you want to point students toward highly ranked journals in AI, here's a list of the top journals as reported by *various citation counts sources* (this list changes year to year):

- o Communications of the ACM

- o Artificial Intelligence

- o Cognitive Science

- o IEEE Transactions on Pattern Analysis and Machine Intelligence

- o Foundations and Trends in Machine Learning

- o Journal of Memory and Language

- o Cognitive Psychology

- o Neural Networks

- o IEEE Transactions on Neural Networks and Learning Systems

- o IEEE Intelligent Systems

- o Knowledge-based Systems

GUIDE TO USING THE CHAPTERS

For each of the chapters, I provide next some various ways to use the chapter material. You can assign the tasks as individual homework assignments, or the tasks can be used with team projects for the class. You can easily layout a series of assignments, such as indicating that the students are to do item "a" below for say Chapter 1, then "b" for the next chapter of the book, and so on.

a) What is the main point of the chapter and describe in your own words the significance of the topic,

b) Identify at least two aspects in the chapter that you agree with, and support your concurrence by providing at least one other outside researched item as support; make sure to explain your basis for disagreeing with the aspects,

c) Identify at least two aspects in the chapter that you disagree with, and support your disagreement by providing at least one other outside researched item as support; make sure to explain your basis for disagreeing with the aspects,

d) Find an aspect that was not covered in the chapter, doing so by conducting outside research, and then explain how that aspect ties into the chapter and what significance it brings to the topic,

e) Interview a specialist in industry about the topic of the chapter, collect from them their thoughts and opinions, and readdress the chapter by citing your source and how they compared and contrasted to the material,

f) Interview a relevant academic professor or researcher in a college or university about the topic of the chapter, collect from them their thoughts and opinions, and readdress the chapter by citing your source and how they compared and contrasted to the material,

g) Try to update a chapter by finding out the latest on the topic, and ascertain whether the issue or topic has now been solved or whether it is still being addressed, explain what you come up with.

The above are all ways in which you can get the students of your class involved in considering the material of a given chapter. You could mix things up by having one of those above assignments per each week, covering the chapters over the course of the semester or quarter.

As a reminder, here are the chapters of the book and you can select whichever chapters you find most valued for your particular class:

<u>Companion Book By This Author</u>

Advances in AI and Autonomous Vehicles: Cybernetic Self-Driving Cars

*Practical Advances in Artificial Intelligence (AI)
and Machine Learning*
by
Dr. Lance B. Eliot, MBA, PhD

This title is available via Amazon and other book sellers

Companion Book By This Author

Self-Driving Cars:
"The Mother of All AI Projects"

by Dr. Lance B. Eliot, MBA, PhD

This title is available via Amazon and other book sellers

Companion Book By This Author

Innovation and Thought Leadership
on Self-Driving Driverless Cars

by Dr. Lance B. Eliot, MBA, PhD

This title is available via Amazon and other book sellers

This title is available via Amazon and other book sellers

Companion Book By This Author

Introduction to Driverless Self-Driving Cars

by Dr. Lance B. Eliot, MBA, PhD

Chapter Title

This title is available via Amazon and other book sellers

This title is available via Amazon and other book sellers

Companion Book By This Author

Transformative Artificial Intelligence Driverless Self-Driving Cars

by Dr. Lance B. Eliot, MBA, PhD

Chapter Title

This title is available via Amazon and other book sellers

Companion Book By This Author

Disruptive Artificial Intelligence and Driverless Self-Driving Cars

by Dr. Lance B. Eliot, MBA, PhD

Chapter Title

This title is available via Amazon and other book sellers

<u>Companion Book By This Author</u>

State-of-the-Art
AI Driverless Self-Driving Cars

by Dr. Lance B. Eliot, MBA, PhD

<u>Chapter Title</u>

This title is available via Amazon and other book sellers

Companion Book By This Author

***Top Trends in
AI Self-Driving Cars***

by Dr. Lance B. Eliot, MBA, PhD

Chapter Title

This title is available via Amazon and other book sellers

Companion Book By This Author

AI Innovations and Self-Driving Cars

by Dr. Lance B. Eliot, MBA, PhD

This title is available via Amazon and other book sellers

This title is available via Amazon and other book sellers

<u>Companion Book By This Author</u>

Sociotechnical Insights and AI Driverless Cars

by Dr. Lance B. Eliot, MBA, PhD

<u>Chapter Title</u>

1 Eliot Framework for AI Self-Driving Cars

2 Start-ups and AI Self-Driving Cars

3 Code Obfuscation and AI Self-Driving Cars

4 Hyperlanes and AI Self-Driving Cars

5 Passenger Panic Inside an AI Self-Driving Car

6 Tech Stockholm Syndrome and Self-Driving Cars

7 Paralysis and AI Self-Driving Cars

8 Ugly Zones and AI Self-Driving Cars

9 Ridesharing and AI Self-Driving Cars

10 Multi-Party Privacy and AI Self-Driving Cars

11 Chaff Bugs and AI Self-Driving Cars

12 Social Reciprocity and AI Self-Driving Cars

13 Pet Mode and AI Self-Driving Cars

This title is available via Amazon and other book sellers

This title is available via Amazon and other book sellers

Companion Book By This Author

Leading Edge Trends for AI Driverless Cars

by Dr. Lance B. Eliot, MBA, PhD

This title is available via Amazon and other book sellers

<u>Companion Book By This Author</u>

The Cutting Edge of
AI Autonomous Cars

by Dr. Lance B. Eliot, MBA, PhD

<u>Chapter Title</u>

This title is available via Amazon and other book sellers

Companion Book By This Author

***The Next Wave of
AI Self-Driving Cars***

by Dr. Lance B. Eliot, MBA, PhD

Chapter Title

1 Eliot Framework for AI Self-Driving Cars

2 Productivity and AI Self-Driving Cars

3 Blind Pedestrians and AI Self-Driving Cars

4 Fail-Safe AI and AI Self-Driving Cars

5 Anomaly Detection and AI Self-Driving Cars

6 Running Out of Gas and AI Self-Driving Cars

7 Deep Personalization and AI Self-Driving Cars

8 Reframing the Levels of AI Self-Driving Cars

9 Cryptojacking and AI Self-Driving Cars

This title is available via Amazon and other book sellers

Companion Book By This Author

Revolutionary Innovations of AI Self-Driving Cars

by Dr. Lance B. Eliot, MBA, PhD

Chapter Title

This title is available via Amazon and other book sellers

<u>Companion Book By This Author</u>

AI Self-Driving Cars
Breakthroughs

by Dr. Lance B. Eliot, MBA, PhD

<u>Chapter Title</u>

1 Eliot Framework for AI Self-Driving Cars

2 Off-Roading and AI Self-Driving Cars

3 Paralleling Vehicles and AI Self-Driving Cars

4 Dementia Drivers and AI Self-Driving Cars

5 Augmented Realty (AR) and AI Self-Driving Cars

6 Sleeping Inside an AI Self-Driving Car

7 Prevalence Detection and AI Self-Driving Cars

8 Super-Intelligent AI and AI Self-Driving Cars

9 Car Caravans and AI Self-Driving Cars

This title is available via Amazon and other book sellers

Companion Book By This Author

***Trailblazing Trends* for
AI Self-Driving Cars**

by Dr. Lance B. Eliot, MBA, PhD

Chapter Title

This title is available via Amazon and other book sellers

Companion Book By This Author

Ingenious Strides for
AI Driverless Cars

by Dr. Lance B. Eliot, MBA, PhD

Chapter Title

This title is available via Amazon and other book sellers

Companion Book By This Author

AI Self-Driving Cars
Inventiveness

by Dr. Lance B. Eliot, MBA, PhD

Chapter Title

1 Eliot Framework for AI Self-Driving Cars

2 Crumbling Infrastructure and AI Self-Driving Cars

3 e-Billboarding and AI Self-Driving Cars

4 Kinship and AI Self-Driving Cars

5 Machine-Child Learning and AI Self-Driving Cars

6 Baby-on-Board and AI Self-Driving Car

7 Cop Car Chases and AI Self-Driving Cars

8 One-Shot Learning and AI Self-Driving Cars

This title is available via Amazon and other book sellers

Companion Book By This Author

Visionary Secrets of AI Driverless Cars

by Dr. Lance B. Eliot, MBA, PhD

Chapter Title

1   Eliot Framework for AI Self-Driving Cars

2   Seat Belts and AI Self-Driving Cars

3   Tiny EV's and AI Self-Driving Cars

4   Empathetic Computing and AI Self-Driving Cars

5   Ethics Global Variations and AI Self-Driving Cars

6   Computational Periscopy and AI Self-Driving Car

7   Superior Cognition and AI Self-Driving Cars

8   Amalgamating ODD's and AI Self-Driving Cars

This title is available via Amazon and other book sellers

Companion Book By This Author

Spearheading
AI Self-Driving Cars

by Dr. Lance B. Eliot, MBA, PhD

Chapter Title

This title is available via Amazon and other book sellers

Companion Book By This Author

Spurring
AI Self-Driving Cars

by Dr. Lance B. Eliot, MBA, PhD

Chapter Title

This title is available via Amazon and other book sellers

Companion Book By This Author

Avant-Garde
AI Driverless Cars

by Dr. Lance B. Eliot, MBA, PhD

This title is available via Amazon and other book sellers

Companion Book By This Author

AI Self-Driving Cars
Evolvement

by Dr. Lance B. Eliot, MBA, PhD

Chapter Title

This title is available via Amazon and other book sellers

Companion Book By This Author

AI Driverless Cars
Chrysalis

by Dr. Lance B. Eliot, MBA, PhD

This title is available via Amazon and other book sellers

Companion Book By This Author

Boosting
AI Autonomous Cars
by Dr. Lance B. Eliot, MBA, PhD

Chapter Title

This title is available via Amazon and other book sellers

Companion Book By This Author

AI Self-Driving Cars Trendsetting

by Dr. Lance B. Eliot, MBA, PhD

This title is available via Amazon and other book sellers

ABOUT THE AUTHOR

Dr. Lance B. Eliot, MBA, PhD is the CEO of Techbruim, Inc. and Executive Director of the Cybernetic AI Self-Driving Car Institute, and has over twenty years of industry experience including serving as a corporate officer in a billion dollar firm and was a partner in a major executive services firm. He is also a serial entrepreneur having founded, ran, and sold several high-tech related businesses. He previously hosted the popular radio show *Technotrends* that was also available on American Airlines flights via their in-flight audio program. Author or co-author of a dozen books and over 400 articles, he has made appearances on CNN, and has been a frequent speaker at industry conferences.

A former professor at the University of Southern California (USC), he founded and led an innovative research lab on Artificial Intelligence in Business. Known as the "AI Insider" his writings on AI advances and trends has been widely read and cited. He also previously served on the faculty of the University of California Los Angeles (UCLA), and was a visiting professor at other major universities. He was elected to the International Board of the Society for Information Management (SIM), a prestigious association of over 3,000 high-tech executives worldwide.

He has performed extensive community service, including serving as Senior Science Adviser to the Vice Chair of the Congressional Committee on Science & Technology. He has served on the Board of the OC Science & Engineering Fair (OCSEF), where he is also has been a Grand Sweepstakes judge, and likewise served as a judge for the Intel International SEF (ISEF). He served as the Vice Chair of the Association for Computing Machinery (ACM) Chapter, a prestigious association of computer scientists. Dr. Eliot has been a shark tank judge for the USC Mark Stevens Center for Innovation on start-up pitch competitions, and served as a mentor for several incubators and accelerators in Silicon Valley and Silicon Beach. He served on several Boards and Committees at USC, including having served on the Marshall Alumni Association (MAA) Board in Southern California.

Dr. Eliot holds a PhD from USC, MBA, and Bachelor's in Computer Science, and earned the CDP, CCP, CSP, CDE, and CISA certifications. Born and raised in Southern California, and having traveled and lived internationally, he enjoys scuba diving, surfing, and sailing.

ADDENDUM

AI Self-Driving Cars Trendsetting

Practical Advances in Artificial Intelligence (AI) and Machine Learning

By

Dr. Lance B. Eliot, MBA, PhD

———

For supplemental materials of this book, visit:

www.ai-selfdriving-cars.guru

For special orders of this book, contact:

LBE Press Publishing

Email: LBE.Press.Publishing@gmail.com